● ● ● Supporting language
and literacy
development in the
early years

Supporting early learning

Series editors: Vicky Hurst and Jenefer Joseph

The focus of this series is on improving the effectiveness of early education. Policy developments come and go, and difficult decisions are often forced on those with responsibility for young children's well-being. This series aims to help with these decisions by showing how developmental approaches to early education provide a sound and positive basis for learning.

Each book recognizes that children from birth to 6 years old have particular developmental needs. This applies just as much to the acquisition of subject knowledge, skills and understanding as to other educational goals such as social skills, attitudes and dispositions. The importance of providing a learning environment which is carefully planned to stimulate children's own active learning is also stressed.

Throughout the series, readers are encouraged to reflect on the education being offered to young children, through revisiting developmental principles and using them to analyse their observations of children. In this way, readers can evaluate ideas about the most effective ways of educating young children and develop strategies for approaching their practice in ways which offer every child a more appropriate education.

Published titles:

Bernadette Duffy: *Supporting Creativity and Imagination in the Early Years*
Vicky Hurst and Jenefer Joseph: *Supporting Early Learning – The Way Forward*
Linda Pound: *Supporting Mathematical Development in the Early Years*
Marian Whitehead: *Supporting Language and Literacy Development in the Early Years*

Supporting language and literacy development in the early years

Marian Whitehead

Open University Press
Buckingham • Philadelphia

Open University Press
Celtic Court
22 Ballmoor
Buckingham
MK18 1XW

email: enquiries@openup.co.uk
world wide web: http://www.openup.co.uk

and
325 Chestnut Street
Philadelphia, PA 19106, USA

First Published 1999

A catalogue record of this book is available from the British Library

ISBN   0 335 19931 3 (pb)   0 335 19932 1 (hb)

Library of Congress Cataloging-in-Publication Data
Whitehead, Marian R.
     Supporting language and literacy development in the early years/Marian Whitehead.
        p.   cm. – (Supporting early learning)
     Includes bibliographical references and index.
     ISBN 0-335-19932-1 (hb). – ISBN 0-335-19931-3 (pbk.)
     1. Language arts (Early childhood)–Great Britain.   2. Children–Language.
     I. Title.   II. Series.
     LB1139.5.L35W53   1999
     372.6'0941–dc21   98-41549
                                                                                         CIP

Typeset by Type Study, Scarborough
Printed in Great Britain by Biddles Ltd, Guildford and King's Lynn

For Natalie, Daniel and Dylan,
and in memory of Vicky

Contents

Series editors' preface

This book is one of a series which will be of interest to all those who are concerned with the care and education of children from birth to 6 years old – childminders, teachers and other professionals in schools, those who work in playgroups, private and community nurseries and similar institutions; governors, providers and managers. We also speak to parents and carers, whose involvement is probably the most influential of all for children's learning and development.

Our focus is on improving the effectiveness of early education. Policy developments come and go, and difficult decisions are often forced on all those with responsibility for young children's well-being. We aim to help with these decisions by showing how developmental approaches to young children's education not only accord with our fundamental educational principles, but provide a positive and sound basis for learning.

Each book recognizes and demonstrates that children from birth to 6 years old have particular developmental learning needs, and that all those providing care and education for them would be wise to approach their work developmentally. This applies just as much to the acquisition of subject knowledge, skills and understanding, as to other educational goals such as social skills, attitudes and dispositions. In this series there are several volumes with a subject-based focus, and the main aim is to show how that subject can be introduced to young children within the framework of an integrated and developmentally appropriate curriculum, without losing its integrity as an area of knowledge in its own right. We also stress the importance of providing a learning environment which is carefully planned for children's own active learning. The present volume shows how listening, talking, reading and writing start from the moment a child is born. The author traces this development in young children, and gives us a great deal of help in learning how to promote and support these fundamental abilities, so that our children not only become good communicators, but develop into lifelong and passionate devotees of all forms of literature.

Access for all children is fundamental to the provision of educational opportunity. We are concerned to emphasize anti-discriminatory approaches throughout, as well as the importance of recognizing that meeting special educational needs must be an integral purpose of curriculum development and planning. We see the role of play in learning as a central one, and one which also relates to all-round emotional, social and physical development. Play, along with other forms of active learning, is normally a natural point of access to the curriculum for each child at his or her particular stage and level of understanding. It is therefore an essential force in making for equal opportunities in learning, intrinsic as it is to all areas of development. We believe that these two aspects, play and equal opportunities, are so important that we not only highlight them in each volume in this series, but also include separate volumes on them as well.

Throughout this series, we encourage readers to reflect on the education being offered to young children, through revisiting the developmental principles which most practitioners hold, and using them to analyse their observations of the children. In this way, readers can evaluate ideas about the most effective ways of educating young children, and develop strategies for approaching their practice in ways which exemplify their fundamental educational beliefs, and offer every child a more appropriate education.

The authors of each book in the series subscribe to the following set of principles for a developmental curriculum:

Principles for a developmental curriculum

- Each child is an individual and should be respected and treated as such.
- The early years are a period of development in their own right, and education of young children should be seen as a specialism with its own valid criteria of appropriate practice.
- The role of the educator of young children is to engage actively with what most concerns the child, and to support learning through these preoccupations.

- The educator has a responsibility to foster positive attitudes in children to both self and others, and to counter negative messages which children may have received.
- Each child's cultural and linguistic endowment is seen as the fundamental medium of learning.
- An anti-discriminatory approach is the basis of all respect-worthy education, and is essential as a criterion for a developmentally appropriate curriculum (DAC).
- All children should be offered equal opportunities to progress and develop, and should have equal access to good quality provision. The concepts of multiculturalism and anti-racism are intrinsic to this whole educational approach.
- Partnership with parents should be given priority as the most effective means of ensuring coherence and continuity in children's experiences, and in the curriculum offered to them.
- A democratic perspective permeates education of good quality and is the basis of transactions between people.

Vicky Hurst and Jenefer Joseph

Acknowledgements

I wish to thank the children, parents and staff of Hampden Way Nursery School, London, and Rosebridge Steiner Kindergarten, Cambridge, for generously allowing me to use their photographs, documents and examples of children's work in this book – especially in Chapter 5 which would not have been possible without them.

My special thanks to Vicky Hurst and Jenefer Joseph, the series editors, for all their affection, wisdom and support. Vicky died during the writing of this book and her loss has been heartbreaking, but Jenefer has remained strong and encouraging.

Warm thanks must also go to Allyson Pascoe, Headteacher of Hampden Way, and Sally Jenkinson, Early Years Adviser, Steiner Education UK, for all their commitment, generosity and guidance.

I also wish to thank for their help and interest the staff, children and parents of: Aylsham Nursery School, Norfolk; Christchurch Gardens Steiner Kindergarten, Reading (Figure 5.9); Earlham Nursery School, Norwich; Hethersett Woodside First School, Norfolk; The Lindens Waldorf Kindergarten, Stroud; Northfields First School, Norwich; Sunlands Steiner Kindergarten, Stroud; West Earlham First School, Norwich; and Wynstones Steiner School (kindergarten), Gloucester.

My loving thanks, as always, to my family who supply so much of the inspiration and examples of language in action and then allow me to write it up.

Introduction

There is no shortage of sound books about language in the early years and the production of yet another calls for a little justification. My first defence is that this book does not stand alone – it is one of a series of books advocating a developmental approach to young children's education. If we are to pursue this approach successfully we must understand the complex nature of children's development in the early years and have a particular focus on communication and language, because they are such very significant features of this picture. So this is a book which presents a developmental view of language and, although that is not so unusual, it goes on to combine in one fairly accessible volume perspectives on the role of literature and the emergence of literacy in the early years. Such a wide-ranging approach to language development is getting less common as the requirements for emphasizing literacy (and numeracy) come to dominate educational practices and publications.

This book covers the age range 0–6 or 7 years, and picks up on the unparalleled speed and complexity of growth in children's thinking, language, social and cultural awareness and physical skills in this period. While looking at this broad phase of child development the book quite consciously challenges the unhelpful gulf, created by haphazard and historical legislation in the UK, between care and education for the under-5s and care and education for the over-5s. This has led to young children's development and language being forced to fit in with such arbitrary arrangements. This book goes to the core of the matter and looks at what appears to be crucial in language development in these early years.

This fresh look at the nature of early language development has led me to reformulate my priorities for language in these early years and focus on: the significance of non-verbal communication; the importance of language play; the roots of emerging literacy; and the notion of language and education as shared community endeavours. There are chapters in the book which address these themes specifically (Chapters 1, 2, 4, 7) but they also permeate the total approach.

The complexity of each of the above priorities means that it is not easy to sort out the implications for parenting and early years pedagogy, or what is often called the study of learning and teaching. In order to be more supportive of parents, carers and educators, I have ended the chapters which look at aspects of language development (Chapters 1, 2, 3, 4) with notes on how to start supporting children's learning and language more effectively. Additionally, at the heart of the book is a chapter written to support and encourage parents and professional practitioners by showing examples of good practice (Chapter 5). This chapter presents a case study of two distinctive approaches to early education, including language, literature and literacy, and although they originate in different traditions (the British nursery school and Steiner Waldorf education) they offer considerable food for thought, not least the idea that if education and care are to be truly democratic and inclusive, they must be allowed to learn from different philosophies of childhood and pedagogy, and even encouraged to celebrate their differences, as well as their common assumptions.

The positive experience of studying and cooperating with these two distinctive 'schools of thought' and their children, staff and parents, led me to the unavoidable critique of national legislation and requirements for language and literacy in Chapter 6. These national frameworks can restrict the kinds of language and literacy experiences educators and professional carers are able to offer young children in group settings. They also narrow the understanding of many untrained providers, and confuse or mislead parents and the wider community. This critique of language policies in the UK is part of the wider concerns voiced by the editors of this series of books (Hurst and Joseph 1998: 4) that early education is now being driven – and distorted – by political expediency and ideology, to the detriment of children and the adults working with them.

But there is still great joy to be found in parenting, caring and educating in the early years and I have attempted to incorporate many examples of children's thinking and language, as well as photographs and pieces of their work. One aim of this book is to enthuse readers, whatever their roles and responsibilities for young children, so that they return refreshed to their hugely important work with young children and treat it as if it were the best possible kind of play. We should strive to find and hang on to the 'wow factor' in all our dealings with young children; I mean by this always being ready to be impressed, amazed and enchanted by them. This is not a 'soft' or romantic option, for it takes courage, intelligence and creativity to understand and respond appropriately to children and take on the role of being challenging partners in their learning.

I have often been told that the best way to read a text is to bring one's own questions to it and make reading a kind of interrogation of the text. Perhaps it will help you to know what questions I had in mind as I wrote this text:

- What might an appropriate language curriculum for the early years look like?
- Are the current national frameworks and requirements likely to nurture successful literacy in the early and later years?
- What can we learn from different approaches and beliefs about early education and the teaching of language and literacy?
- What can parents, carers, educators and local communities do to support language development in the early years?

This book is not in the business of providing foolproof answers, but it does hope to provoke a lot more questions and a lot more thinking about language, literature and literacy.

1

Great communicators

The setting is a fine spring evening in a Cornish seaside town. A young couple with a child of around 12 to 15 months are sitting by the harbour. The child's buggy has been positioned as close as possible to the railings along the harbour wall and the child is leaning forward and gazing intently down at the rising tide, pointing at the lapping water, feet kicking excitedly, shouting 'sea', 'sea', 'sea'. The mother responds by saying 'Yes, it's the sea' several times.

It is all too easy to assume that an interest in children's language development must start with an interest in words and how children learn to use them. In the course of history many parents and scholars have believed just that and waited impatiently for infants to say their first words. Some legends suggest that an emperor with a taste for language study actually conducted an experiment to see if the first words of some unfortunate babies he had kept in isolation would be Latin! Even modern albums of the 'our baby' type, used for recording a child's development, usually include a page for 'first words'. But if we really do wish to understand more about language and support its development in childhood we need to start much earlier: we have to look at what is going on in the first hours and days after birth and not be misled by the excitement of words. Words rest on foundations that are laid down in the earliest communications between babies and their carers.

Communicating

For generations parents and carers have sensed that their newborn infants are attentive, playful and friendly, and modern research now supports such intuitions with clear evidence. It would seem that babies are great communicators from birth and have a range of pre-programmed abilities (instincts) which enable them to form close relationships with their carers. For example, babies prefer to look at human faces and eyes and pay attention to human voices. They actually spend remarkably long periods of time just gazing into the eyes of their carers (Schaffer 1977; Stern 1977). The recipients of this adoration are normally entranced and respond by smiling, nodding, talking and stroking the child's face, especially the cheeks, chin and lips. To an observer this behaviour can look remarkably like a real conversation, with turns taken to speak and gaps left for the 'speechless' baby to slot in comments. The adult partner behaves 'as if' this were a conversation and the slightest blink, squeak or squirm from the child is interpreted as a meaningful communication. But the infant partner is also very discriminating and will only give this level of attention to people. Although moving objects are tracked and watched, it is familiar adults who are usually treated to smiles, speech-like lip movements and arm waving (Trevarthen 1993). Furthermore, babies can set the pace for communications, making eye contact when they are feeling alert and sociable and dropping their gaze when they no longer wish to play this early language game. All these abilities are illustrated in Figure 1.1, as 12-week-old Dylan enjoys a relaxed conversation on the bed with his father. The photograph has captured the remarkable mirror image between the partners: their eyes are locked in a mutual gaze and even the shaping of their lips and the opening of their mouths are synchronized. The movement of Dylan's right arm suggests that he is conducting the pace and duration of this particular conversation.

Continuing research into the sociability and communication skills of babies has demonstrated that they can imitate some interesting adult behaviours within minutes of birth (Trevarthen 1993). The list of actions imitated includes mouth opening, tongue-poking, eye blinking, eyebrow raising, sad and happy expressions and hand opening and closing. Perhaps it is not too fanciful to see these actions as crucial ones in the life of a social being who will live in groups, small and large, and communicate face to face by means of voice, expressions and gestures. We cannot dismiss these earliest acts of communication as insignificant flukes; clearly they are pre-programmed (in the genes) and therefore of some survival value to our species. Furthermore, adult carers solemnly imitate their

Figure 1.1 Dylan (12 weeks) and dad communicating.

babies and go along with the agendas they set. All this has been observed in recent years by professionals as varied as anthropologists, psychologists, linguists and educators, and the fascinating business of baby watching has attracted popular attention too (Morris 1991). There appears to be general agreement that early communication between babies and carers is a non-verbal form of 'getting in touch' with another person and crucial in the development of language, as well as of understanding and sympathy with others, and of social skills, cooperation and play.

In their earliest communications with a human partner babies also learn about themselves and how others see them. As they gaze into the eyes of their carers they see a mirror image of themselves and the responses of carers indicate how unique, human and loveable their infants are. This mirroring (Winnicott 1971), if it is a good experience, is the foundation of the child's own self-esteem and ability to love and inspire affection, and is yet another indicator of the significance of this period in a child's development when powerful communications take place without words.

Communicating babies and their carers do not live in vacuum packs and the worlds of particular cultures and communities shape their gestures, expressions, movements, talk and songs, so that from the start a baby enters a culture as well as a language. The basic patterns and timetable of language development are universal, but the fine details of gesture, talk, song and traditional care and beliefs about infants are as varied as the languages children learn. This is an important reminder that the roles of carers, families and cultural communities will always be of great significance in children's linguistic, intellectual and social development. Children do not just learn a language, they learn a way of life.

The kind of communication discussed so far is described by linguists as 'non-verbal communication': it helps to prepare babies for speech and underpins our use of spoken language for the rest of our lives. This word-less communication can also develop into sophisticated signing systems for the deaf, as well as complex signalling systems for occupations as different as dance and mime, racecourse bookmaking and aircraft landing control. The main characteristics of non-verbal communication in infancy are:

- face-to-face intimacy;
- strong feelings (from warm affection to rage and frustration);
- very dramatic use of facial expressions, especially eyes and eyebrows, mouth, lips and tongue;
- whole body movements (including dancing, for example), head nod-ding and shaking, arm and hand gestures;
- the use of 'mouth sounds' like clicks, whistles, hums, 'raspberries' and loud 'boos'.

The last set of characteristics may seem a little bizarre, but we all make use of 'tuts', grunts, 'mms' and even whistles in our talk, especially on the telephone when we have to keep in touch with our invisible talk partner. In the early days of infant communication, imitating these exaggerated mouth sounds may help the baby to practise a whole range of sounds used in the eventual production of words, but we should also note that such sounds may by funny, outrageous and even rude. Right from the start there is a strong current of playfulness, mucking about and teasing in com-munication – and babies do as much of the mucking about as do their carers (Reddy 1991; Trevarthen 1993). This teasing is a kind of fibbing, or playful deception, and is thought by some linguists to explain partly how language originated. In group life it was (and still is) important to be able to influence others, guess what was in their minds, and even 'change their minds'. Apparently the great apes, our nearest animal relatives, are 'extremely skilled deceivers' (Aitchison 1997: 26) – especially the chim-panzees – but for purely selfish reasons often connected with food. Human beings, however, can choose to tell a lie which is kind rather than brutally honest, and have turned fibbing into games (see Chapter 2) and 'telling tales' into an art form (see Chapter 3).

Finding the words

First words, when they come, do not spring perfectly formed after months of silence. As examples of meaningful sounds, they emerge from babbling which has been strongly influenced by the sounds of the language, or languages, used constantly with and around the child. As understandable and regularly used labels for people, objects, feelings and events, they can be traced back to the early months of non-verbal communication, when babies develop recognizable 'sounds' for significant people, toys and noisily impressive objects like lorries and aeroplanes. These personal labels evolved by an infant may start out as a 'gaa' or 'brr' but they gradually move closer to the standard words used in the home and speech community (Halliday 1975). In the course of this development they are often 'stretched' in their use by the child so that they can cover a whole range of similar events or ideas. For example, the sound or word for 'car' may be used for lorries, shopping trolleys and lifts; the early word for a significant male carer or parent may be used for any man seen in the street or on the local bus.

This gradual building up of a collection of important words for things is greatly helped by the behaviour of carers who communicate with babies and play the sorts of games which involve highly predictable routines with their own special sounds and words. For example, simply giving and taking things and saying 'please' and 'thank you', or waving and saying 'bye-bye', or pointing at and naming things in homes, streets, magazines, catalogues, picture books and on the television screen. All these important language games really get things going, but words are not just any old random sounds and identifying the first words of immature speakers is not easy (after all, they will have difficulty forming certain sounds for some years in early childhood). Because of this, modern linguists, unlike proud parents and carers, have a set of criteria for what is really a 'first word':

- it is used spontaneously by the child;
- it is used regularly in the same activity or setting;
- it is identified by the carer.

The emphasis on spontaneous use is important because with first words we are looking for evidence of the child's ability to identify and attempt to share meanings by using words – we are not interested in the skills of a well-trained parrot! The best evidence for meaningful word use is the child's reusing of the word in appropriate and similar situations. Treating the carer as the expert who can recognize and identify these first words is essential because only a regular carer has intimate knowledge of the child, as well as detailed knowledge of the contexts in which early words emerge.

The expertise of carers and the contexts in which children use their first words are interesting features of early language learning. Many studies of first words have been conducted and later published by linguists working with their own children – or their grandchildren (Engel and Whitehead 1993) – because carers are best placed to understand their children and their settings. This very powerful insider knowledge has revealed, among other things, that first words start as personal but highly consistent sounds (Halliday 1975); that first words are vivid records of the home life, culture and experiences of children; and that toddlers continue to practise language – especially new sounds, rhymes and words – on their own before falling asleep (Weir 1962; Nelson 1989).

Children's first words indicate how they are sorting out and making sense of their particular worlds and they also provide a guide to what really matters to them. When collections of first words are analysed it soon becomes clear that they can be grouped under such headings as: members of the family, daily routines, food, vehicles, toys and pets (Whitehead 1990). Clearly, people, food, animals and possessions are of great importance to babies and their obvious attractions drive the infants' search for labels. Having the right words for people and things is an almost foolproof way of getting others to help you get hold of, or stay close to, good things.

Also found among the first words are some simple instructions and requests such as 'up', 'walk', 'out', 'gone' and those really important little words in any language, 'yes' and 'no' (or their linguistic equivalents). All these kinds of words enable a small and fairly immobile person to manage other people, get help and make personal needs and feelings felt. During this 'first words' phase of language development it is obvious to parents, carers and professional linguists that children's single words frequently stand for quite complex sets of meanings, communications and instructions. A word like 'dirty' can in certain situations mean 'my hands are dirty', 'are you putting my paint-splashed T-shirt in the washing machine?' or 'I've dropped my apple on the floor'. Only the carer who is with the child at the time can understand and respond appropriately to such one-word utterances – and may still get them wrong! Human communication is always a sensitive and risky business and single words can only do so much. In order to unlock more of the power of language the young communicator must put words together in meaningful and unique combinations.

The power of language

Once young children begin to combine words together it is even more obvious that they are thinking for themselves and have some powerful understanding about how languages work. The evidence for these big claims can be found in the children's unique language creations which cannot have been imitated from adults and older children. We are likely to hear such requests as 'door uppy' (open the door) and 'no doing daddy' (don't do it daddy), and older infants go on to create new verbs out of nouns, as in 'lawning' (mowing the lawn) and 'I seat-belted myself' (putting on a seat-belt). Professional linguists get very excited about these examples (although other people often dismiss them as 'funny things children say') because they are evidence that all children are born with an innate ability to understand and produce appropriate and meaningful language (Chomsky 1957; Aitchison 1989; Pinker 1994). In fact, this remarkable ability to combine words together so that they make sense is grammar in action and indicates that a child is capable of thought, as well as able to be sociable and influence others.

Professional linguists describe 'grammars' in terms of the things they enable us to do with language (this may come as a surprise to readers reared on a strict diet of adjectives, past participles and the like) and the two highly significant functions of language are: getting things done – especially with the help of others – and commenting and reflecting on the world (Halliday 1975). Young children certainly use their emerging skills as speakers in order to get carers and others to do things for them ('chair uppy': lift me onto the chair), and they also make statements which suggest that they can observe the world and comment on what happens ('no more miaow', said as the cat leaves the room). It is worth emphasizing that these early word combinations are evidence of thought, and of an innate ability to share and communicate meanings. Many people are convinced that language is for communication and socializing, which it is, but they overlook its role in our thinking and memory. Yet there is powerful research evidence, as well as common sense, to tell us that language creates and extends our ability to think about abstract and complicated ideas such as 'trust' and 'freedom', or things that are distant in time and space (dinosaurs; Australia; last week's visit to the cinema; my first taste of ice-cream), as well as the entirely invented and non-existent 'little green creatures from Mars', Paddington Bear and Jane Eyre.

These are examples of language as a symbolic system – that is, a way of letting words stand for things, ideas and experiences even in their absence, so that we can hold onto them and think about them. This is so central to human thinking that in cases where disease or genetic damage impair or prevent the development of speech and language other symbolic systems must evolve. The signing and touching 'languages' used by the deaf and the blind provide ways of sorting, ordering, recalling and reflecting on experience as well as gaining the cooperation of others. In early childhood the developmental patterns of affected children may show some personal and some general variations. The emergence of grammatical understanding will be in the normal range because it is pre-programmed and universal, but early word acquisition may show some delay (Harris 1992) because it is triggered and enriched by all the social and cultural naming and labelling games played with babies. It is important that infants who do have some form of sensory impairment have endless opportunities to touch, feel, move rhythmically, sign and name all the people, objects, materials and animals in their environments. We can still learn a great deal from the inspired teacher who placed the hands of the blind and deaf Helen Keller under a gushing water pump and constantly wrote the letter signs w-a-t-e-r on the child's palms as the water poured over them. Such support was left almost too late for Helen Keller who had to retrieve years of loneliness and frustration, but every impaired infant can be helped from the start with a range of stimulating sensory experiences linked to words or signs.

A *timetable for speech and language*?

In many ways learning languages never stops: we all increase our stock of words and continue to pick up the latest technical terms and fashionable slang of our groups and cultures. Many children start with more than one language, particularly in multilingual societies, or go on to acquire a second and third language at an early age. Some adults learn a new language for professional or social reasons, even to enhance their holidays in foreign countries, and schools in most societies are required to teach one or more other languages. The process of becoming literate and learning the written system of a language is also part of language learning, as is the skilled way in which we all adjust our language (dialect) and our pronunciation (accent) according to particular situations and audiences. But the earliest stages of learning to speak in childhood hold a great fascination for most adults who work with children and/or raise their own families, and some kind of developmental timetable is often asked for. However, such timetables can be rather dangerous if taken too seriously and interpreted with rigidity. Every child and every set of circumstances into which she or he is born is different, which renders timetables both unhelpful and potentially worrying for parents and carers. It is for this reason that no such timetable is included in this book.

A *few notes on grammar*

Some comments on grammar in this chapter may have seemed strange and require a brief explanation. A great deal of ignorance, prejudice and even fear surrounds the topic of grammar, and the modern study of language – known as linguistics – has not really changed this. The problems arise because there are two very different views of grammar, although few people understand or admit this. The most widespread view is rooted in largely discredited beliefs about what is 'correct' and 'good' in language and emphasizes traditional rules of thumb which tell us how we *ought* to speak and write. This is known as the 'prescriptive' tradition because it 'prescribes' or 'tells us' exactly what the users of a language *ought* to do. However, the rules prescribed are mainly based on examples from Latin (historically the language of a very few educated and scholarly groups) and from written language, neither of which provide helpful guidance for young contemporary speakers of a living language, or their families. This rather illogical approach is aggravated by a general fear of change and of the ethnic and linguistic diversity in society, plus an excessive and persistent respect for privileged groups whose private education still values classical, 'dead' languages highly. This is sometimes at the expense of living languages which are caricatured as having no grammar and not best suited for training the mind. Of course the situation is rarely described in such blunt terms, but the damage such unchallenged assumptions can do is considerable.

For example, the prescriptive approach has the effect of dividing a society into those who believe that they speak correctly and those who become convinced that they are bad speakers of their first language. It also promotes a rather nasty view of languages as ranked in league tables with some – mainly English and western European languages – at the top because they are supposedly more logical and sophisticated. This approach not only dismisses some languages (and by implication their speakers) as primitive and limited; it also seriously undervalues their young speakers' remarkable and creative achievements in early language learning.

The study of modern linguistics presents a quite different approach to grammar and actually sees it as a universal feature of human thinking, thus providing us with clues about how the mind works. The essential difference in approach stems from the fact that this linguistics is 'descriptive' not 'prescriptive', and aims to describe how we actually learn to speak and the rules we appear to be following when we speak and write a living language. In order to do this modern linguists attempt to be *scientific*: they look at what is going on in every aspect of language use. So, they observe, record, analyse and make informed guesses about what is happening in a language and what individual speakers and groups are doing with language in any given situation. They certainly do come up with rules for how a language works, but they get the rules from what speakers and writers are *doing* with language and they are always ready to change their descriptions over time as a language changes to meet the needs of its speakers.

Educators and carers need to understand a little about what lies behind the endless arguments about language and grammar, if only to realize that the disagreements are like the old quarrels between flat-earthers (a bit like prescriptive linguists) and those who accepted that the earth was round (somewhat like descriptive linguists)! The serious point here is that guidance and statutory regulations for the teaching of language, grammar and literacy are being imposed on early years settings, schools and even parents, and some of these regulations are very prescriptive and closer to a 'flat-earther' position than is admitted. For example, a long list of words to be learnt and recognized out of context are prescribed in the *National Literacy Strategy: Framework for Teaching* (DfEE 1998) for Reception year children, and these words are not memorable ones like 'elephant' or 'banana', but include the likes of 'and', 'my', 'it', 'was', and so on. Further lists of 'high frequency' words are also provided for the rest of the primary years. Chapters 3 and 4 will indicate more sensible, enjoyable and properly language-based approaches to helping young children build up their abilities to recognize such words on sight.

In conclusion, we need to be proud of young children's language, thinking and early literacy behaviours, and able to defend a sensible descriptive view of languages. We can point out that modern grammar is not an undisciplined free-for-all, but describes the rules of a language operating on at least three levels concerned with:

- the organization and patterns of *sounds* (known as phonology);
- the meaningful *combination of words* (known as syntax);
- the *meanings* of words and groups of words (known as semantics);

A fourth level, the *vocabulary* or stock of words in a language (known as lexis), is often included in grammatical descriptions.

This description of several levels of grammatical rules highlights the skill and complexity involved in the everyday use of language by any speakers and the remarkable achievements of young children in learning languages. However, it is not an easy guide to teaching grammar – in most cases these rules are far too complex for direct teaching – but it is a kind of ground plan for basing our approaches in the early years on children's love of language, their desire to communicate and their need to make sense of life and experiences. If simple rules are required, then we could do no better than suggest:

- raising the status of *talk* and *communication*;

- ensuring that any language use, spoken or written, is *appropriate for its purpose and situation*;
- drawing children's attention to print everywhere and *making print exciting*.

Supporting young communicators

Successful caring, parenting and educating is bound up with paying close and serious attention to young children and helping them to understand their world and manage themselves in it. But taking children seriously as people does not have to be grim and humourless – on the contrary, the best adult carers and educators are the most playful. The child watching the rising tide at the start of this chapter was already at the single-word naming stage of communication, but she (or he!) had been supported just enough to make talk about the sea possible: the buggy was as close as safety allowed to the edge of the harbour wall so that the child could peer down; time was made for uninterrupted watching; the child's recognition and naming of the sea was taken up by the mother and confirmed and expanded into a fuller statement. Above all, the sheer joy of watching the sea was communicated and shared. We can assume that this kind of communication had been repeated in other settings and circumstances many times before and had developed out of months of child and adult play, subtle body language, adult talk and shared communicative sounds and gestures.

We have to value all the non-verbal interactions which occur between infants and adults (or older children) in homes and group settings, create extra opportunities for them, and continue to value a wide range of non-verbal communications after spoken language is established. This will be particularly crucial for children whose first language is not English when they enter care and group settings, because they have to depend on picking up all the non-verbal communicative clues they can. The challenge this presents for the professional adults working with these young potential bilinguals can, however, lead to a wonderful freeing up and transforming of the procedures and curriculum in the setting.

Provision and activities

The following will help ensure rich linguistic beginnings:

- *People* Play, talk and interaction with other people are the key activities at this stage. At home, parents, other family, siblings, child minders and nannies are the key provision. In group care settings, key workers or stable carers for the youngest babies; a wider number of adults, young adults and older children, as well as same-age peers (babies who are able to sit up enjoy the company of other babies).

- *Places* In group settings some very small rooms and sheltered areas, inside and out, with cushions, carpeted areas and blankets to lie and sit on; the creation in homes and institutions of safe cupboards, dens (tables with floor-length drapes/cloths over them) or full-length curtains to hide behind; safe garden houses, trees, bushes and improvised tents (blankets, sheets and clothes-airers), and even sturdy fencing to peep through or imagine what lies on the other side.

- *Things to do* Face-to-face gazing, talking, gesturing, bouncing, singing, dancing, clapping; opportunities for listening and quiet watching (other children and adults, animals, moving trees, mobiles, out of windows, pictures, books); plenty of 'helping and talking' activities like food preparation, clearing up and domestic chores, bath times, getting dressed, gardening, shopping, walks and visits; opportunities to play with collections of natural and manufactured objects presented in 'treasure baskets' (Goldschmied and Jackson 1994) (e.g. wooden and metal spoons, fir-cones, shells, sponges, containers and lids, balls); also, saucepans and lids, rattles, squeakers, simple percussion instruments, wooden and plastic blocks (building bricks), soft toys and dolls; a small collection of picture, story, poetry and alphabet books.

- *Things to talk about* All the above provide ample opportunities for communication and talk and the development of complex forms of thinking.

Further reading

Campbell, R. (1996) *Literacy in Nursery Education*. Stoke on Trent: Trentham Books.
Hall, N. and Martello, J. (1996) *Listening to Children Think: Exploring Talk in the Early Years*. London: Hodder & Stoughton.
Tizard, B. and Hughes, M. (1984) *Young Children Learning: Talking and Thinking at Home and at School*. London: Fontana.
Wells, G. (1987) *The Meaning Makers: Children Learning Language and Using Language to Learn*. Sevenoaks: Hodder & Stoughton.
Whitehead, M. (1996) *The Development of Language and Literacy*. London: Hodder & Stoughton.

2

Play and language

The family are having dinner and 7-year-old Daniel overhears his grandfather saying to another adult, in an aggrieved tone, 'I'm doing my best'. Daniel glances mischievously at his sister and then says with exaggerated politeness to his grandfather, 'Did you say "I've ruined my vest"?'. At this point both children giggle helplessly.

Contradictory as it may seem, this chapter will attempt to get serious about play and look more closely at what is going on when young children muck about with whoever, or whatever, comes to hand. Perhaps we recall a baby who has wriggled under its blankets and inadvertently caused the rattles strung across its pram or crib to shake musically. In no time the infant is engrossed in finding ways of moving so that the rattles shake on demand and this can soon lead to bashing them with energetic sweeps of the hands. An older infant who is more mobile will discover that bunches of keys can be shaken to produce sounds; saucepans can be banged and clashed, 'drunk' from in a pretend way, or even worn as hats! Toddlers will talk to soft toys, picture books and cushions, or pretend to be windscreen wipers, monsters and crying babies. Groups of 3- and 4-year-olds will create elaborate dramas about such themes as space, holidays, weddings, hospitals and jungles, and begin to delight in nonsense words, verses and slightly rude ideas and language. And the safe and confident 6- or 7-year-old can make fun of grandad by echoing the rhyme and the rhythm of his speech, but changing the words, as Daniel did. This game with language is played by children whenever songs, hymns or commercial jingles are given newer and ruder words: '*Neighbours, pick your nose and taste the flavours*' (from a south-east London Reception class).

If we try to distance ourselves from these very ordinary examples of playful behaviour in infancy and early childhood by looking at them as if for the first time, we may be struck by their remarkable features. So let us imagine what an observer from Mars would record about the young human (note that our Martian visitor uses the term 'things' for people, events and emotions, as well as objects):

- Things are not always what they seem: a cushion can be a baby; a dark corner can be a cave; a child can be a cat; and a child who is misrepresenting an adult's words may be praised.
- Things can be changed: a cooking pot is a headdress, a cup for non-existent drink and a percussion instrument; a simple chair can also be used as a ladder or a launch pad for flying leaps.
- Things can be controlled: accidental sound effects can soon be repeated to order by a baby who finds ways to move rattles and mobiles; the anger of adults can be managed and dispersed by jokes and laughter; adult attention and help can be organized by infants using cries, smiles and words.
- Things can be repeated and practised: infants repeat movements which bring pleasure or new sensations; certain stories, songs and words are listened to and said again and again by young children; children also imitate the behaviours and appearance of some animals, people and objects.

Our Martian observer would have to conclude that these goings on must be of great significance for the human species and would not be surprised to learn that the study of many kinds of playful behaviour is an important ingredient in modern academic work in psychology, linguistics and literacy. We might also expect our galactic visitor to ask to see the curriculum arrangements for such an important activity as play in our education systems! The following sections could prove useful if the Martians do arrive to study play, language and the human animal, and might also make a difference to families, early years group settings and curriculum planners.

Play and players

There has been a long tradition of explaining play, but in western and Anglo-Saxon cultures it has tended to be regarded as a bad habit which has to be exposed and perhaps excused. This has persisted and coloured modern attitudes to young children and to their schooling and we must all be aware of the distinctions made between play and work in most adults' minds. In the UK this has resulted in a national curriculum that does not have a view of play or a policy for it and official 'outcomes' for the education of pre-5s which are equally lacking in any real understanding of play.

Traditional views of play tended to describe and explain what purposes it might serve from the perspective of the species, and so the suggestions covered such possibilities as using up excess energy, repeating some developmental features of human evolution, or practising skills which would be essential to adult life. Modern approaches look more closely at the individual who is playing and try to capture the flavour of what it feels like to be playing, as well as the purposes of the player. There is some room in such studies for the older concerns with practising skills and most contemporary scholars emphasize the long and vulnerable childhood of the human individual and the need for close and mutually satisfying relationships with carers (Bruner 1976). Perhaps the major differences in modern approaches are, first, the emphasis that is put on the child as an active player from birth who initiates and even choreographs the dance of communication and play with carers (Reddy 1991; Trevarthen 1993). Second, a keen awareness of the role of play in infant communication skills and early language, and in a most significant form of human thinking – the symbolic.

These are very complex ideas, and an everyday example might help:

> The tube train I am travelling on stops at a station and an Asian couple with a toddler in a buggy get on (I can only guess that the child is around 18 months old). The train is fairly crowded and the man stands while the woman sits and places the buggy so that the child can face the man. The little girl fixes her carer with a very 'smiley' gaze and begins to go through a remarkable and silent performance: first she waves her right hand in a vertical up and down gesture, the man smiles and responds with the same wave. Next the child waves in a horizontal left-right, right-left movement and the man responds by copying this. The next trick in the little girl's repertoire is to slowly drop her head onto first one shoulder and then the other, all the while maintaining steady eye contact with her male carer. Clearly these intimate and endearing communication games have been played and developed over some time, but the child is not entirely unaware of the people around her in the train. Another female passenger begins to wave back to the child and try to catch her eye and this eventually breaks the spell between child and carer. At this point the child is both fascinated, wary and shy and resorts to peeping at the stranger from under the basket on the handles of the buggy and then twisting round completely to gain eye contact and reassurance from her female carer.

In this incident we see the child confidently in charge of starting and leading all the little communication games with her carers. In contrast, we
also see how she is confused and wary when a stranger breaks in on the
performance. The gestures and body language are examples of human
symbolic behaviour and, like adult handshakes, nods and smiles, they
stand for particular meanings in particular communities. Symbols always
stand for something: they are more than they seem because they carry
meanings.

Symbolic thinking is a powerful and economic way of thinking and
understanding almost anything and is essential when we need to think
about difficult and abstract ideas which cannot be touched, tasted or
pointed to – ideas like 'loyalty' or 'distance', for example. We need some
kinds of shared symbols if we are to share with others our feelings and
ideas – just as the toddler on the noisy and crowded tube train needed to
assert her security and identity by rehearsing her rituals of attachment
with her carer. We also need the symbolic systems of languages, pictures,
movements and so on if we are to communicate about what is far away, in
the past, or total fantasy. The solution to these difficulties is to let something – the symbol – stand for ideas, objects, feelings, events and so on.
And symbols can be many things: the words of a language, a baby's
special sound for a toy or person, a gesture, a uniform, a bunch of flowers,
a drawing, a religious ceremony or a national anthem. Our whole lives are
spent creating, using and responding to symbols and our babies begin the
process at (or soon after) birth, when they fill their relationships with
carers and objects with emotion and feeling, so that blankets, breasts or
feeding bottles are more than objects – they are security, relationships,
identity and a sense of worth (Winnicott 1971). It is in this way and at this
early stage that our names and the sounds of our languages take on a
special life and feeling for us. Similarly, wider experiences increase the
symbolic resources and thinking of young children so that soft toys are
cuddled and loved, the shadowy space under the table becomes a cave
and a long stick can easily be a horse to ride. An early introduction to
stories and rhymes will extend the experiences and thinking of children by
offering new symbols to use in the form of fictional characters, activities
and situations (see Chapter 3).

Play in childhood and in adult life creates a kind of space and time where
we can try things out without having to match up to external notions of
correctness and can take risks. During play we can get to grips with things
which matter to us alone, build new relationships with other people and
even take time out to do nothing at all. Players of any age are typically
engrossed in their play and although we often hear that play must be
defined as pleasure or enjoyment this should not be taken to mean that
smiles and laughter accompany all play. Play can be deeply thoughtful

and challenging, or it may explore emotions such as anger, pity and sadness. Careful observations of young children playing reveal that they struggle to build a tower of bricks, try to divert waves into a sandcastle's moat, or play at being dead (Almon 1997). What we can say about young players is that they have set their own tasks and challenges, are 'supposing' about the chances of life, and finding useful symbols to play and think with. They are also investigating their world, being creative and flexible, and learning. Because how they feel about the things they are doing is central to play, they are also developing emotionally. This latter point is now taken very seriously by modern psychologists who deplore the damage done to children by narrowly academic kinds of education which originated in the nineteenth century and are a hopelessly inadequate preparation for twenty-first century thinkers (Gardner 1991; Goleman 1995; Claxton 1997). The issue here is the danger of missing out on children's extraordinary potential for all kinds of thinking and feeling if families, early years group settings and schools ignore or undervalue play and the development of the full range of human intelligences. Intelligence is not just a single ability to solve problems by mathematical logic – there is also musical, linguistic, bodily, artistic and interpersonal intelligence, to name but a few.

Play with language

Language and play share several characteristics: both use symbols to stand for a range of ideas, feelings and experiences; both are reflections of human thinking and also creators of new thoughts; both are part of our genetic make-up. Language is also one of our first playthings in infancy and remains an important play area for us, long after we have given up mud pies, rattles and dolls. The following examples are focused on early childhood but will indicate the persistence of play with language into adulthood.

Play with language can be simplified for the purposes of discussion by dividing it into two broad aspects: play with the matter, or stuff, of language, and play with the meanings encoded, or expressed, in language. The stuff of language is sound and there is little doubt that very early language play begins when babies – often helped and copied by their carers – gurgle, blow 'raspberries' and bubbles, squeal, grunt and babble. Babbling is a form of rhythmic early mouth play with the sounds of what will become a language, and is usually accompanied by bouncing, rocking and arm and leg pulsing movements. The pleasure and ease of babbling, repeating the same sounds in the same parts of the mouth and throat, still satisfy us long after we have given up babbling. So we sing 'la-la-la' or 'doo-bee-doo' to our favourite tunes; chant rhythmically at sports matches, rallies and demonstrations; or admire the scat singing of jazz musicians. As children mature and have wider social experiences they learn to chant over and over again the simple tongue-twisters, taunts and street raps of their communities. Such favourites as 'she sells sea shells on the sea shore' and 'cowardy, cowardy, custard' are rather thin on deep meanings but are rich examples of repeated sound patterns and rhythms.

Children are very sensitive to rhyming sounds in their languages and it is no coincidence that the traditional literature of infancy and early child-hood is rhyming verses, notably the nursery rhymes of the Anglo-Saxon cultures. Rhyme can be complex but a simple definition is the occurrence of matching or identical sounds in words or in the end sounds of lines of verse:

Humpty Dumpty
Sat on a wall
Humpty Dumpty
Had a great fall

If rhyme draws our attention to the end sounds of words, alliteration works by choosing identical or similar beginning sounds, as in tongue-twisters like 'Peter Piper picked a peck of pickled peppers'. Rhythm, rhyme and alliteration are the basic tools of the poet and the songwriter and they make it very easy to remember lines and whole verses. They would have been important memory aids in non-literate societies and they still work for pre-literate young children and busy adults who want to hang on to the words and rhythms of a favourite song or verse.

One other important form of play with the stuff of language is the simple pleasure of repeating favourite words or phrases over and over again. This can be a child's reaction to the beauty and strangeness of newly-found words and I have memories of one small girl who was enchanted by the word 'strawberry' and shouted it aloud for days. Many adults still cling to childhood snippets which may be reassuring but are no longer conveying literal meaning, as with phrases like, 'goodnight, God bless', or just 'bless you'. But the real culmination of all this play with the material of language is the art of poetry – yet poetry is far from being a series of enchanting sounds empty of meaning, and we need to look at play with the meanings of language.

Young children encounter new words all the time and although the meanings of many words are fairly obvious in the context in which they are met, we are sometimes made aware by a child's misunderstanding that we do use some ordinary words in extraordinary circumstances. This usually happens when words have taken on some extra symbolic functions and become metaphors – that is, we refer to complex and abstract matters 'as if' they were something commonplace and everyday. Perhaps my explanation has not 'hit the nail on the head' (a metaphor), but the following example may 'grab you' (another metaphor):

> The situation is a family picnic on a village green in the Norfolk Broads. Several exotic-looking ducks are asleep under the surrounding bushes and I remark to my 7-year-old grandson, Daniel, that they are 'ornamental' ducks introduced into Britain. A group of visitors arrive and feed the birds on the nearby river and our sleeping ducks wake promptly and move off to the river bank for their share. Daniel shouts excitedly, 'They're not ornamental, Marian. They're moving, they're moving!'

Clearly Daniel understood just one literal meaning for 'ornament' until I used the word metaphorically, and this is how the slow process of acquiring complex word meanings proceeds. Often an experience of this kind is followed by lots of playful and experimental trying-out of the new word meaning. A Russian scholar noted a little girl describing a piece of stale cake as 'middle aged' (Chukovsky 1963) and a 3-year-old of my acquaintance was wildly excited when he first heard the word 'trip' used to mean an outing of some kind. Up to then he had only used it to mean a fall, so he drove us all a little weary by staggering round giggling and elaborately pretending to trip over paving stones while shouting constantly: 'He's going on a trip today!'

The clowning reaction of this little boy reminds me that there is considerable research evidence from other cultures that children between the ages of 2 and 4 delight in nonsense and turning their newly-learned language upside down (Chukovsky 1963). This same research suggests that nonsense verse and silly jokes are very popular with young children because the craziness of it all helps them to sharpen their own grasp on reality and assert their own superiority to characters who go to sea in sieves or burn their mouths with cold porridge! One other very significant finding from Chukovsky's study was that attempts to suppress young children's playful and exploratory thinking and language use by imposing adult information and realism were totally ineffective. This should be remembered when early years provision and an appropriate curriculum are being planned.

The 'play way' to literacy and phonics

There was a fashion in the early decades of this century to name reading schemes – which were usually phonics-based – as if they were pathways to rapturous joy and happiness, so little children skipped along 'gay' ways and 'radiant' ways to the promised land of literacy. My own small contribution to this tradition is to claim that children are more likely to become enthusiastically literate if play with the sounds and the literal and metaphorical meanings of language is taken seriously in the early years.

The whole issue of phonics and alphabet knowledge has received a great deal of publicity in recent years and families, carers and early years educators are under considerable pressure (some of it statutory and political) to follow misguided advice. This arises because so many people have a simplistic understanding of language, literacy and human thinking and believe that traditional phonics, which started by teaching one sound matched to one letter of the alphabet, can help with reading English – a language which happens not to be very consistent at the level of representing sounds. People will earnestly claim that they learnt to read this way, but they are clearly unaware of all the other experiences, complex skills and insights which came together as they learnt to read.

It is a fact that modern psychologists and linguists have studied young children's sensitivity to rhyme and alliteration, their knowledge of nursery rhymes and their recognition of letters of the alphabet. These researchers do not talk about traditional phonics as described above, and refer to their work as research into children's *phonological awareness* and *alphabetic knowledge*. Their research suggests that pre-5s who have considerable informal experience of sharing rhymes, songs, alphabets, picture books and daily routine talk with carers are already sensitized to language and literacy and likely to make an early start on reading (Bryant and Bradley 1985; Hasan 1989; Goswami and Bryant 1990).We do know that English-speaking children's reading development is closely connected with their knowledge of rhyme. In Chapter 1 there is a reference to research in the USA which gathered evidence that very young children alone in bed at night spontaneously practise new words and phrases and create their own sets of nonsensical and standard rhyming and alliterative words (Weir 1962; Nelson 1989). It is likely that this sensitivity to the rhythms and sound patterns of language is a universal feature of all cultures and their languages, as songs, poems, dances and music from around the world all indicate. So perhaps infants are 'wired' for rhyme and word-play from the start (McArthur 1995) and we should concentrate on making the right connections with them and for them.

Supporting play with language

Making the right connections for infants and young children depends on the willingness of carers, families and educators to understand and encourage the highly exploratory way in which their children handle and test out all new experiences. This really does mean *all* experiences: from getting to know new people to finding out what can be done with a dish of cereal; from trying to work out whether 'no' really means 'no' to checking how securely a sibling's hair is attached; and from trying out a series of 'knock knock' jokes on a carer to inventing names for new cities created on a software program.

Within this context of supporting early learning through play and experimentation carers and educators have another responsibility: to share with children all the many ways in which a community and a culture play with language. This is a simple matter of introducing young children to rhymes, songs, music and dance steps, sayings and proverbs, chants, advertising jingles, poems, jokes, puns and tongue-twisters, and so on. But this is not a matter of formal contracts to do 'play with language' once or twice a day for ten-minute sessions. It would be disastrous and as ineffective as giving newborns lessons in communication and language acquisition, or enrolling 1-year-olds for correct walking tuition! We know that play with language, particularly rhyming, is a powerful predictor of successful early literacy, but it is so just because it is part of what it means to be human and to think in linguistic and symbolic ways. The best pre-literacy lessons happen at home with parents when bathing infants and changing nappies, washing and peeling vegetables, singing and dancing to the tape/radio/television, making the beds or unloading a basket at the supermarket checkout (see below). Many of these activities can also be done in group settings and professional carers and educators should avoid using such oddities as 'sound tables' and phonic lists. The source of phonological knowledge is the human voice – people talking, singing and playing with languages (several if we are lucky).

Provision and activities

- *People*   Parents, stable carers and key workers to begin with, widening out to members of local families, communities and ethnic groups to encounter other languages, songs, rhymes and poetry; exposure to a range of accents and/or dialects; use of tapes, radio and television to broaden language listening and joining-in experiences; group settings can contact poets, storytellers and folk-singers for visits; regular contacts with other infants, toddlers and children – lots of play with language and learning new words, songs, rhymes, etc., including the mildly naughty, happens in peer groups.

- *Places* Everywhere! (Homes, shops, buses, clinics, group settings, schools, playgrounds, parks.) The note on 'Places' at the end of Chapter 1 is equally appropriate here as small, sheltered and 'secret' spaces provide the safe and intimate settings we all need in order to take risks with play and with language.
- *Things to do* All the activities listed under this heading at the end of Chapter 1 provide the essential beginnings of play with language. Add: *bathing and nappy changing* – child and carer blowing bubbles and making other mouth sounds (clicks, 'raspberries', humming); repeating names of child and carer, turning them into a rhythmic song, adding actual and nonsensical words which rhyme or are alliterative; doing the same for names of pets, soap, nappies, bath toys, cream, clothes, etc.; accompanying these games and songs with bouncing, rocking, leg and arm waving, tickling, water splashing, saying 'boo', whistling, finger-clicks.

Washing and peeling vegetables – adapt most of the above suggestions, singing rhythmically as the water runs into the bowl (simple chants such as 'we're washing carrots, we're washing carrots, they look like parrots, they look like parrots'); find another rhythmic chant for the peeling action; talk about what other fruits and vegetables are the same colour; list all favourite foods and all most disliked foods; if you find making up songs and chants difficult or a child is reluctant to do so, just sing nursery rhymes, folk and pop songs or commercial jingles. (My father sang cockney music-hall songs to me and so from an early age I could warble 'boiled beef and carrots' and 'my old man said follow the band' – some excellent rhymes and alliteration in this kind of material!)

Unloading a supermarket basket – again, adapt all the above ideas. Of course singing and dancing round the checkout can be disruptive, so wait until you get back home or to your early years setting. However, items can be named as they come out of the basket, names can be repeated and alliteration and rhymes can be emphasized. This is a good chance to look at packaging, pictures, logos and letters. Pick out any initial letters that are the same as those of the child's name (this will soon lead to the child noting these letters all over packages, posters and buildings).

Start a small collection of published alphabet books; use paper or scrap books to begin to make alphabets for children, sticking on pictures, photos and children's drawings, but let the children choose the items (we can get away from 'A for apple, B for ball' and go for avocados and balti).

Personal alphabets can be made at home and in group settings. Think about a collection of nursery rhyme and poetry books to share on a daily basis; early years settings can convert their 'sound tables' into poetry tables and corners; record the child/children singing their favourite chants, songs, rhymes, poems, jokes, etc. (made-up, traditional or modern) so that they are available on tape for listening and singing together sessions.

Play with language may seem silly and slightly subversive but it is intellectually stimulating for children and the foundation for literacy and further language learning.

Further reading

Beard, R. (ed.) (1995) *Rhyme, Reading and Writing*. London: Hodder & Stoughton.

Chukovsky, K. (1963) *From Two to Five*. Berkeley, CA: University of California Press.

Gardner, H. (1991) *The Unschooled Mind: How Children Think and How Schools Should Teach*. London: Fontana.

Paley, V. G. (1981) *Wally's Stories: Conversations in the Kindergarten*. Cambridge, MA: Harvard University Press.

Opie, I. and Opie, P. (1959) *The Lore and Language of Schoolchildren*. Oxford: Oxford University Press.

3

Once upon a time

> Once there was a magic circle in the forest and a giant lived inside.
> There was a boy and his sister walking into the forest. The giant tried
> to trick them because if you stepped inside the circle you turned into a
> spell. But he couldn't trick them so they went home and had supper.
> (Paley 1981: 66)

This storyteller is a 5-year-old black American boy called Wally who has
taken to dictating a vast number of tales to his kindergarten teacher.
Wally's stories seem to pour out of him in response to the daily events,
people, feelings and puzzles of his life, at home and in the kindergarten. In
this instance the story appears to have been inspired by a large circle
painted on the kindergarten floor by the teacher, to create a simple stage
for the children's dramatic improvisations. The remarkable thing about
Wally's story is its familiar traditional ingredients: two vulnerable little
children alone in the forest; the danger posed by a powerful giant; the
courage and wisdom of the little children; and their safe return to home
and supper.

This story is a remarkable achievement, but it is not an unusual one –
stories, both mundane and fantastic, are made up and told by children of
all ages, and by adolescents and adults. It seems that we are all born storytellers and our tales can be about our inner lives and emotions ('how we
feel'), our current state of health ('how we are'), our religious beliefs and
moral values ('what we believe'), our loyalties to families, cultures and

nations, ('who we are and where we come from'), or they can be rework-ings of all the other stories we read, hear and see ('what we have learned'). The prevalence of stories in our lives makes them of great interest to psy-chologists, psychiatrists, doctors, priests, politicians, journalists, artists and scientists. This can be rather a surprise to people who think that stories belong just to children, novelists, entertainers and English teachers, but there is a particular reason for early childhood educators and carers to take an interest in human story making and story sharing: it seems that we actually think – to a large extent – by using stories, and our memories are organized as a series of stories.

A simple demonstration of this is to ask someone what sort of a day they have had; usually their response is in the form of a set of edited highlights from that day. The highlights seem to be selected because they matter to the teller, but also because the teller judges them to be of some interest to the listener. So our audience and our setting shape these personal stories and help the teller of any age to mull over events and feelings and judge their significance. In fact, so important are our stories to our thinking and our feelings that we tell them to ourselves, as if we had some kind of inner listener who was always there. Of course, very young children will not always tell their stories verbally, although they certainly talk to themselves a great deal. They act stories and dance them, they draw or paint them, mould them in mud, sand and clay, or even beat up a favourite teddy! So, what is a story?

What is a story?

A story is any number of happenings, real or imaginary, which have been organized so as to be told or shared in some form (words, songs, dances, ceremonies and rituals, cave paintings and so on). The organizing system for stories is known as narrative and it provides a kind of backbone for all the stories we hear, see and tell. One very straightforward definition of narrative emphasizes the fact that it is always about 'telling': *'Someone telling someone else that something happened'* (Smith 1981: 228).

Here we have the most crucial and basic of all language activities. We hear it when a carer soothes a baby with a little story of how nice their trip to the clinic will be, or when a child in the nursery tells us about her mishap with the watering can. We also hear it in ancient legends, histories, poems and folk tales, as well as in modern novels, biographies and daily gossip. Yet, although we find these narratives everywhere, there is nothing random or sloppy about narrative tellings, and two essential character-istics identify a narrative: a concern with time and a concern with values.

A concern with time

A narrative is a sequence of events ordered in time, so that at its simplest we get the events of a story told in the order of their happening and linked by such language as 'and then . . . and then . . .'. Many carers will be familiar with a young child's account of a day at the playgroup which goes like this: 'I showed Mrs X my new gloves and then I played with the sand and then I went on the swing and then I sang "The Wheels on the Bus" and then it was home-time'. Teachers of older children in Key Stages 1 and 2 of the National Curriculum will have noticed that this same basic narrative form is used by them in their early attempts at lengthy pieces of writing. It certainly is a wonderful device for spinning out a long oral story, a juicy piece of gossip or a lengthy written narrative. The long narrative in Appendix I was written over the ten days of a Christmas holiday by brother and sister Daniel (7 years 1 month) and Natalie (9 years 11 months). It was inspired by imaginative play with a collection of toy bears and the main author was Daniel, but Natalie took over as scribe when Daniel tired, and sometimes contributed to the plot. The division into chapters, the adventure theme and the 'blurb' on the back of the cover indicate how much the children were influenced by their knowledge of books and the patterns of the narratives they had heard and read since infancy.

The concern with time in narrative also indicates its links with the organization and functioning of human memory: 'When I was three and Bailey four, we had arrived in the musty little town, wearing tags on our wrists which instructed – "To Whom It May Concern" – that we were Marguerite and Bailey Johnson Jr. , from Long Beach, California, en route to Stamps, Arkansas, c/o Mrs Annie Henderson' (Angelou 1984: 6). This kind of storytelling and writing is like a mental diary which is constantly added to and revised and reminds us of who we are and what has happened to us. From the earliest years we have to know these things if we are to manage our lives and form satisfactory relationships with others.

A concern with values

Narrative is just as much concerned with human values as with time and this brings out the issue of selection and choice of what to tell and what to leave out. This is as important for the hearer or reader as it is for the teller and stories are enjoyed for the clues they give about the values, attitudes and judgements of the narrator(s). We may not agree with the values in a narrative, but we do add them to our stock of knowledge about people and about the chances of life. How often have you summed up a bit of gossip, or a strange story from the media, with a folk-saying such as 'There's nowt queerer than folk' – as my Lancastrian mother-in-law would say? Narrative is a very important method for speculating on life and human behaviour and is not restricted to great novels and plays, as familar sayings, proverbs and gossip indicate. It is an essential tool for all of us, but especially so for young children who often feel confused and vulnerable and have to find out a lot about people and life in as short a time as possible.

Community narratives

Throughout our lives we use narrative selection, ordering, telling and evaluating to give patterns, meaning and predictability to what would otherwise be random sensations and happenings. The evidence for this comes from communities and cultural groups as well as from individual development. The narratives of whole communities are usually stories which explain the origins, beliefs, history and moral values of the group and they are familiar to most of us as myths, legends, folk tales, rhymes, proverbs and sayings. All of these would once have been part of an oral (spoken) tradition existing long before the development and spread of writing and printing. Much of the traditional literature we share with young children – for example, nursery rhymes, lullabies, nonsense, folk and fairy tales – is really ancient and full of the accumulated wisdom of many generations. Hence the little bits of folk-warnings we may recall from childhood: 'it will all end in tears'; 'never cast a clout until the May is out'; 'you made your bed and you must lie on it'.

However, this wisdom is not entirely in the past and groups and cultures still continue to make sense of their lives and pass on their experiences to their children. We now do so less by word of mouth, and instead use the media, organized schooling, churches and popular entertainment. For young children, these community narratives are significant introductions to the shared beliefs, values and meanings of their cultures. Most of us are comfortable with such cultural symbols as Paddington Bear, Anansi and Cinderella for discussing behaviour and moral viewpoints, but there is evidence that young children are eager to make sense of the most up-to-date media narratives. Television news bulletins have been found to pre-occupy 2- to 5-year-olds in Australia, as their attempts to make sense of them with their own retellings indicate:

Sara, 5:   I saw that. Princess Diana crashed and she got squashed.
Bekky, 5:   When she was getting buried, she was in a thing [makes a square using her fingers] with flowers on top.

(Weddell and Copeland 1997: 1)

Community narratives must deal with both the terrible and the joyful happenings in life and very young children need to talk about and play at funerals and crashes, as well as superheroes, weddings and space monsters. They also need to create narratives about their own identity, relationships and feelings.

Personal narratives

Researchers make very strong claims about the importance of narrative in personal development. It has been described as a primary function of the mind (Hardy 1977) and a kind of 'brain fiction' (Gregory 1977). Brain fictions are all the possible strategies or scenarios which we try out 'in our heads' before risking real action. Telling ourselves stories about 'what may be the case' is an instance of what is more grandly known as 'forming hypotheses' and this makes human thinking very much like scientific behaviour.

We need to be aware that very young children are constantly finding themselves in the same situations as research scientists: they are frequently meeting new events and happenings and trying to create stories which predict the most likely outcomes and offer explanations. Scientists' stories or hypotheses advance human knowledge; children's stories enable them to survive and cope with life, as well as adding to their personal store of knowledge. Listen to Mollie who is 2 years and 11 months as she struggles to do the right things in kindergarten: '"I'm not too big to reach that", she says, trying to hang up her jacket. "But my already birthday is going to come now. Then I can be big to reach it."' (Paley 1986: 4). Or eavesdrop on some 7-year-olds investigating a pair of broken spectacles found in a box of historical objects:

Sharon: It could have been the old man's and when he died, something could have happened to them to get broke . . . something could have fallen on them.
Claire: Well the Romans could have knocked his glasses off and cracked them.
Children: [Several] No.
Josh: The old man wouldn't be alive. The old man wasn't alive when the Romans were here.
Kath: He would have been 2000 years old.

(Hoodless 1996: 114)

The stories these children from nearly 3 to 7 years old are narrating help them to deal with abstract ideas and difficult problems, and provide them with theories of life which can be modified and improved in the light of experience and new information.

The first two chapters of this book have emphasized how carers first tell their infants little tales about their appearance, mannerisms and personalities, and how personal storytelling and language play develop in 2-year-olds. From this stage children increasingly use in their own narratives the cultural sayings, songs and stories that they are told, see on television or overhear. Such expressions as 'once upon a time' or 'there was once a baby who got lost' or 'they all lived happily ever after' remind us that young storytellers are already beginning to sound more like books and have in fact begun to use orally the language of literacy. This really is one of the true basics of literacy. Babies and young children who hear plenty of oral stories and stories from books and television, and share in meaningful talk with adults and other children, become tuned-in to the broad patterns of stories and the language and ways of thinking found in our written systems.

A *curriculum is a story*

This chapter began with Wally telling a story about the latest event in his kindergarten class, but it would not be correct to think that his narrative skills were just an accidental bonus for his teacher. In fact the teacher, Vivian Gussin Paley, built her early years curriculum on the children's narrating activities. She did this by audio recording *all* the daily talk and narrating that went on, and used this material as her guide to the children's current interests and knowledge, their questions and curiosity, and the first signs of new interests and queries. Her analysis of the children's daily narratives shaped her forward planning of activities and provision, as well as giving her insights into the children's individual all-round development and enabling her to make appropriate interventions and provide the right kind of support. She also reflected deeply on her own role and the purposes of early years education as she listened to the stories her children were telling.

Wally and the big painted circle incident tell us that mutually respectful talk between children and between adults and children, as well as story, rhyme, poetry, plays and dramatic re-enactments were the core of this particular narrative curriculum. But any curriculum is a kind of story, although it may not be as supportive of young children's learning as the Paley variety. A curriculum is a small selection, or story, chosen from all the thousands of possible things we could tell our children from our accumulated knowledge and experience. As such, like any narrative, it reveals a great deal about what a particular human group values and cannot bear to leave to chance in the passing on of information, beliefs and attitudes to the next generation. Our curriculum choices also show what we think will be absolutely essential for the survival and prosperity of our children, so for the last few hundred years developed countries have emphasized literacy and numeracy in any type of organized schooling, but not fishing, hunting and the building of simple shelters. Of course these skills may still be valued and taught by some families, clubs and groups.

The dominant curriculum stories in contemporary British schools and early years settings are about literacy and numeracy, along with narratives of our history (very selective and partial), plus some tales of the natural world and the human environment. This is an important reminder for all who work with young children – particularly in school settings at Key Stage 1 and the start of Key Stage 2 – that the only satisfactory way for children to understand the subjects of the National Curriculum is through stories. We have to set the facts of science, technology, geography and history, for example, in the contexts of stories about how people live and solve problems now, in the past or in distant places. Similarly, we may tell stories of how animals survive and adapt, or introduce children to stories about the nature of materials and the universe we inhabit. This is not that difficult when we realize that human beings have always told stories which explained the pattern of the seasons, the shapes and locations of the star constellations and how the camel got his hump! What is difficult is having the courage to let the children work through and play with their own early explanatory stories – because they will certainly be creating them. Given time, respect and encouragement they will do what we all do: gradually modify their own personal theories with more and more of the 'facts' set down by tradition and experts. The alternative to this process of gradual assimilation is the unwise one of imposing facts on young children who, because they cannot make human sense of them and have nowhere to put them, dump them as soon as possible. This is unacceptable in terms of wasted educational opportunities and lives. Good early years carers and educators should always be telling manageable tales about the facts, from digital technology to multiple addition.

However, there is more to a curriculum than the facts, or subjects, we choose or are required to tell about. A curriculum includes 'all the learning opportunities' offered in a school or early years setting; 'all the behaviour that is encouraged or discouraged; the organisation and routines; the way adults, including parents, interact with the children' (EYCG 1992: 16). In other words, it is not just what you tell that counts, it is the way that you tell it. This involves the respect we show to children, the opportunities we provide for learners to make their own sense of our curriculum stories, and the chances they have to contribute to the curriculum. A backward-looking curriculum which only tells about some facts and values which suited a vanished world cannot help children to think and be socially and intellectually adaptable in the twenty-first century. Our children need a foundation early years curriculum which nurtures strong self-esteem, the ability to form loving relationships of many kinds, respect for the diversity and common humanity of others, a sense of social responsibility and the potential to think independently, creatively and flexibly. This may appear to be a very tall order but there are sound reasons to believe that a curriculum with play and literature at its core may deliver these good things (Heath 1997), *plus* the literacy and numeracy we all desire for our children.

The following section provides some advice for carers and educators who wish to begin, or develop further, the telling of tales to young children and goes on to discuss some important types of literature and books for babies and young children.

Telling tales

Telling tales, as distinct from reading books to children, is an ancient and central human activity and still has the power to enchant audiences of any age. The ability to tell a story, no matter how short, is the educator's and carer's best life-saving kit! The tale can be a brief illustrative example of how not to 'wash' a lettuce, or about how big a dinosaur would have appeared if it stood in our local supermarket/park/high street. A spontaneous story can be made from a richly rambling account of what the teller's schooldays were like in rural Pakistan or Wales, or inner-city Baltimore or Belfast. Fantastic worlds of monsters, space aliens, little pigs, wizards, gods, monkeys, ghosts and abandoned orphans can also be conjured out of the air if we remember and share the tales we all heard in our own childhoods.

How to tell tales

The first instruction, and the most important, is: enjoy yourself! This means that you must enjoy the story you plan to tell and believe that it is really worthwhile. This means that you should try to plan and rehearse your stories, including any little 'warm-ups' and any follow-up activities. Rehearsing a story means knowing where the crucial events in the plot occur and giving them plenty of emphasis. It also means knowing just how you will handle the climax and how you will end your tale. None of this involves learning 'off by heart' or being word perfect because every telling will be slightly different, in response to the setting, the audience

(1 child; 20 children; in bed; in a playgroup; in a classroom) and the emotional mood. The things we need to plan ahead are the *bones* of the story – the flesh will grow with each telling.

The second instruction is: enjoy the language! Spoken language is at the heart of your telling and needs to be enjoyed for its actual sounds, rhythms and repetitions. Plan for lots of repeated phrases, no matter how daft! My grandchildren can never get enough of the ritual opening of every story my husband tells them: 'When I was a lad, not much bigger than Leila is today . . . ' The joke is that Leila is their pet cat. Try to build in little jokes and nonsense, or snippets of songs, alliteration, rhymes, foreign words and playful mispronunciations, or whatever form of language play appeals to you and your children.

The third instruction is: enjoy the performance! Good storytelling is a performance and some acting skills are required, but it is more relaxing if you think of it as having the courage to make a fool of yourself. Your voice and your body are the means for communicating the story and they enable the child/children to understand and share it. This means using your voice in different ways to outline the plot events, set out the moral and emotional values of the narrative and describe the characters. All this can be done by changes of pitch and volume and a well-planned use of pauses. Characters can be identified by using different accents, styles and registers for them. Remember that regular eye contact with your listeners and your facial expressions, gestures, mimes and body language can also tell a great deal of the story and keep the listeners enthralled.

The fourth instruction is: help your listeners to enjoy themselves! Listeners need to feel secure and comfortable and should be reasonably close to the storyteller. In small groups and families this is not a problem with a baby or small child in the carer's arms or snugly held on their lap, but large group settings and schools can also get round the difficulties by sitting children in a semicircle. Listeners must also be invited into the story and this is why well-planned opening routines, or the 'warm-ups' mentioned above, are so important. After all, a story is a turning away from everyday concerns and demands; it creates a space in which we contemplate life, explore new ideas and take some emotional risks – we may meet Wild Things, or get locked in the house! Some tellers like to make the break with everyday reality by singing a repeated phrase: 'It's storytime, it's story-time, sshh . . .' (Medlicott 1997). Some like to play a simple musical instrument like a pipe or a hand drum; others sing and use 'body music' (rhythmic hand clapping, finger clicking, thigh slapping, knee tapping, tongue clicking and so on). Other traditions include sitting in a special chair or wearing a special hat, shawl or jacket, and showing objects associated with the story (a magic pot, a shopping basket). All these ideas make storytelling time special, as well as holding the interest of the audience and guiding their responses. Furthermore, they can still be used and developed when reading stories from books is planned.

Final words: none of these special plans for storytelling should stop any of us from spontaneously telling a good tale when the moment is right, whether at bathtime, in the checkout queue, or over a family meal.

Books and literature in infancy and early childhood

Babies and books

Babies' books made of cloth, plastic or strong board are a kind of toy which has been around for a very long time and this reflects a widespread belief that babies born into a literate culture should have books as soon as possible – even in the bath. But books as books, rather than toys, have been shared with very young babies by some families for decades, although these families were usually academics, librarians and booksellers. What we might call 'bookish people'! Many of these families recorded and studied their infants' encounters with books and provide stunning evidence for the early literacy progress and emotional maturity of children who meet books when they are babies (White 1954; Butler 1979; Jones 1996). The important point to be emphasized is that these families were *not* attempting to teach their babies to read in any formal way; they were parents and carers who loved books and literature themselves and wanted to share what they valued so highly with their children, almost literally from birth. We have to imagine the loving, intimate and secure settings in which these babies gazed at pictures, touched the print, gurgled responsively, bounced up and down with the rhythms of poetry, alliterative phrases and catchy rhymes, and probably sniffed at the smooth pages and covers of their favourite books, or sucked the corners. All these experiences would take place while the baby was calm after a feed, or securely held in a carer's arms, or feeling unsettled and needing comfort, or perhaps too wide awake to sleep, and in one rare case suffering great pain (Butler 1979). This strong emotional tone of comfort, well-being and security is never lost but becomes part of a reader's sense of total concentration on a book and temporary withdrawal from the demands of the world. Many adults and children 'switch off' from everything else when they read and prefer to read in such secluded places as the bath, in bed, under tables or behind curtains.

It seems that these special lessons about the pleasures of reading are best learnt in infancy, particularly if we want children to love books and reading rather than just learning to read because someone else says they must. As a result of the growing awareness of the huge advantages and pleasures for carers and babies of book-sharing, attempts have been made in recent years to help more families introduce books and story reading to their babies. This started with a carefully monitored pilot scheme in Birmingham which was organized through the local health visitors and the libraries (Wade and Moore 1993). 'Bookstart' packs containing a picture book, a poetry card, a poster and an invitation to join the local library were given free to the parents/carers of 300 9-month-old babies in the city. This project was not aimed just at bookish families and covered a wide ethnic, social and economic cross-section of the city. The questionnaires which the families filled in at the start of the scheme and after six months revealed that the joys of book sharing soon affected the whole family and this included toddlers, older children and adults. In some cases it also led to joining the public library and buying books. A follow-up study of the original families showed that long-term enthusiasm for books had been sustained and the children spent longer periods of time with books and parents/carers (Wade and Moore 1996). The most recent report about these children who started statutory schooling in the autumn of 1997 indicates that not only are they well ahead in speaking and listening and reading and writing, they are also ahead in mathematics (Wade and Moore 1997). It seems that really early experiences with books have given them good insights into numbers, shapes, space and measurement and the researchers attribute this to the counting games, rhymes, shapes and numbers in many children's books. This exciting work, along with similar schemes, has now been extended to many areas of the UK.

We may take away from this kind of research a greater respect for the abilities and potential of babies and the commitment and contributions of their parents and carers to the pleasures of early learning. Babies' earliest experiences with books may have a huge influence on their later attitudes to books and literature, and on their development as readers, writers and learners in the widest sense.

Traditional literature

Folk-fairy tales

At the start of this chapter 5-year-old Wally told a tale of a dark forest, magic spells, a dangerous giant and vulnerable little children. This story is a kind of summary of many of the traditional European folk and fairy tales we share with young children and, along with nursery rhymes, this material has become the literature of the early years of childhood. At first glance this seems strange because the content is very outdated, often cruel and frightening and full of beliefs we no longer accept. Yet the tales and the rhymes appear to be indestructible: they enthrall young children; they have a strange hold over adults who remember them; artists and writers compete to produce their own versions; and modernized retellings of them abound.

What we now describe as fairy tales are in fact a group of ancient folk tales which were written down and made a little more polite and respectable for the French aristocracy's entertainment at the end of the eighteenth century. Along with other collected tales they became popular in the nurseries of the nineteenth-century wealthy middle classes of Europe and America. They were increasingly seen as suitable for children because little moral guidelines had been added to them, but they were already a long way from their origins. These 'folk-fairy' tales began as the pre-literate oral stories of the folk, or common people, and had been told by adults round the fires, in the fields and along the highways. They were not directed at children particularly, but aimed at all the community, so their original themes dealt with the problems, emotions and ambitions of adult men and women. This is why they still have echoes of terrible rage and jealousy (e.g. *Snow White* or *Sleeping Beauty*), early deaths, remarriages and unhappy step-parents and half-siblings (e.g. *Cinderella*), and the horrors of crop failure, starvation and the abandoning of children (e.g. *Jack and the Beanstalk* or *Hansel and Gretel*). All the magic in these old tales can be thought of as a kind of communal wishful thinking and day-dreaming, not that different from the plans so many modern folk make for the day they hope to win the lottery.

There are a number of approaches to explaining the endless appeal of folk-fairy tales and anything goes – from full-blown Freudian analyses (Bettelheim 1976) to Marxist and feminist theories (Zipes 1979). But for the early years educator the 'anything goes' potential of the tales is the clue to their value. In the minds of young children the themes and characters of folk-fairy tales become all-purpose flexible symbols for whatever the child wants them to stand for at any one time. It is a bit like having stories made of Playdough which can be stretched, shaped, pummelled and re-formed as necessary, although they never become shapeless blobs (like Play-dough) but spring back to be the tale they always were! This availability and elasticity also applies to the story settings: they are never too specific (a forest, a cottage, a far-off land) and the time is always an unspecified past – long ago or once upon a time. Characters are often known only by their occupations and characteristics (e.g. a brave woodcutter or a wicked queen), or have names which tell us about their appearance and behaviour (e.g. Goldilocks or Cinderella). Importantly for young children, most of the main characters are small, poor and vulnerable, and survive by a combination of courage and wit, with the help of magical talking animals

or superhuman carers who always turn up just at the right time. It is interesting that some of the worst enemies are huge people (giants and ogres),
terrible hungry beasts, cruel step-parents and witches, or characters who
set the young child/pig/billy-goat mind-blowing riddles to solve. Without being too fanciful ourselves we can see that strange and unpredictable
adults may seem like giants and psychoanalytic studies suggest that
young children do fear being eaten (adults may say playfully, 'I'm going
to gobble you up'). Parents who deny their children things, or become
angry with them, are best seen by the temporarily rejected child as not
their 'real' parent and a witch can be an angry and unacceptable version of
mother (see Anthony Browne's illustrations for *Hansel and Gretel* 1981). As
for the riddles and mysteries, life must seem like that for much of the time
when you are under 7!

The tales of ordinary folk can be found in all cultures, and they tell of our
universal struggles to provide food and survive (e.g. *Bringing the Rain to
Kapiti Plain*, Aardema 1981), to rear our children and see them happy in
adult relationships (e.g. *Mufaro's Beautiful Daughters*, Steptoe 1987), or to
cope with our own greed and folly (e.g. *Brother Eagle, Sister Sky*, Jeffers
1991).

Myths and legends

Myths and legends are also a long-surviving group of traditional stories
and there are some beautifully illustrated and well-written versions being
published. Myths and legends are more than the common stories of a pre-
literate culture – they are the religious explanations of how the world
began, how human beings were created and what kind of relationships
existed between them and their gods, and how the human species relates
to natural creation. These are huge themes and myths do carry the belief
systems of a culture, so that in a multicultural society they are particularly
significant. Legends tend to be more focused on outstanding human
heroes and heroines, especially those who are great leaders of their people.
But legends are not always about kings, queens and emperors – they often
tell of rebels who defy gods or kings in order to protect and help common
humanity (e.g. Prometheus, Ram and Sita, Robin Hood, Superman).

The references above to superheroes are a reminder of how significant
these are in young children's play, drama, drawing and story writing. It
seems that young children do need to try out the feelings of having great
power – after all, for much of the time they are powerless and vulnerable
while adults exercise control over them (and how often do we attempt
to explain our actions and decisions to young children?) Furthermore,
legends and myths raise the moral dilemmas and religious questions we

all have to answer and early exposure to them in exciting story form should be at the heart of our moral and religious curriculum. The great value of myths and legends in a multicultural society must be the access they give to the core beliefs and traditions of many groups. For young children, opportunities to hear and act out the creation stories of many cultures, or explore their relationships with their gods and the natural world, or share in the stories behind their festivals, may set the tone for a lifetime of openness towards people with different backgrounds and beliefs.

Nursery rhymes

The origins of nursery rhymes are incredibly diverse and often argued about, but the good side to this is that they have no official versions and are open to being altered and adapted by adults and children. Some of the rhymes are ancient and predate the spread of literacy; others are snippets from old song books, political satires, plays and religious writings. In common with most of the traditional literature we use with our young children, nursery rhymes were not originally intended for the family nursery and playroom (with the exception of a few verses – for example, 'Twinkle, twinkle, little star', written by Jane Taylor in 1806 – which are not anonymous and were published for children). The best-known traditional rhymes still have reminders of their origins in ballads, folk songs, church rituals and prayers, drinking songs, street cries, wars, rebellions and romantic lyrics. Generations of children must have picked up these verses as their families sung them and generations of carers must have rocked and comforted restless babies with the catchy little tunes and rhymed verses which were in circulation. The fact that these were the 'pop songs' of whole communities explains their gusto, humour and cruelty, for they reflect a world of rough courtships, whippings and heavy drinking and no amount of Victorian 'cleaning up' has fully disguised this.

An important aspect of the appeal of this material for young children is its wild excesses and cruelties. The children can sing about terrible behaviour, and even enjoy the shock value of doing so, while also feeling some sense of how unacceptable it really is to slit someone's tongue, throw an old man down the stairs or drown a cat in a well. Another dominant theme is, of course, nonsense and the previous chapter suggested that play with language and ideas helps children to understand and manage the realities of their lives. By simply turning things 'on their heads' children can test how they work and how far they can be stretched. The far-fetched jokes and nonsense of nursery rhymes are very similar to young children's own humour and may strengthen children's hold on 'what is what', 'who is who' and 'where is where'. After all, young children soon work out that only complete idiots go to sea in sieves, comb their hair with the leg of a chair and burn their mouths on cold porridge, while even a city child knows that cows do not jump over the moon. The stupidity of so many characters in nursery rhymes must be a great morale-booster for children who already know that they would not be so daft as Simple Simon who went whale-fishing in a bucket.

There are many other themes and preoccupations in nursery rhymes, from the difficulties of managing naughty children who go out to play at night, steal pigs and scorch their new clothes to the adult problems of courtship and having too many children. But the most enchanting feature of them is their song-like rhythm and rhyme, and this musical quality ensures that the terrible 'goings-on' are distant and unthreatening, while the words and tunes are highly memorable. Nursery rhymes are rather like a very special kind of toy which children can take over and play with – sometimes to bounce and dance to, sometimes to muck about with the language, and sometimes to explore ideas about what is forbidden, naughty, frightening or just plain puzzling.

Traditional literature puts children in touch with their cultural past and is a unique example of the rhythms and poetry of spoken language. It also contains symbols which are in tune with the emotional and social concerns and anxieties of young children.

Picture books

The modern picture book is the most exciting and challenging aspect of children's literature and artists, writers and publishers almost fall over themselves to be involved in picture books. The linking of picture books with babies and non-readers has often obscured their literary and educational qualities, but there is no excuse for this misunderstanding now that there are many superb and highly sophisticated picture books available for older children and adults. The fact that picture books have 'grown up', and gone 'up market' is partly due to the new technologies of colour printing and book production, but it is also affected by our increased psychological knowledge of just how complex the skills of reading pictures and combining picture meanings with textual (print) meanings really are.

The apparent simplicity of the picture book is also the reason for its complexity because the very lack, or sparsity, of words means that the reader must work very hard to create the narrative from all the clues provided by the pictures. And pictures can show many things happening at once, so lots of choices and decisions have to be made by picture-book readers of any age. For example, *Rosie's Walk* (Hutchins 1968) teases the reader by telling one very simple story in the text and telling a much more dangerous and comical story in the pictures. The sophisticated artwork in such books as *Where the Wild Things Are* (Sendak 1967) and *The Bear Under the Stairs* (Cooper 1993) contains humour, anarchy and tenderness as well as ambiguity about such matters as what is real, what is imagined and what will happen next. It takes many rereadings to get to grips with all these layers of possibilities and it seems that very young children and adults can find new readings every time they return to the pictures. This understanding that picture books are complex and challenging has led to a huge increase in the academic study of them and much of this work indicates that they have an important part to play in the development of early literacy.

The significance of picture books for literacy may be summarized in the following ways: first, they require that very young children behave like active readers. This means that picture book readers must work out, or theorize, from the title, pictures and words what the plot is likely to be about (wild things, bear under the stairs, peace at last); hunt for the main characters (where is the green parrot, where's Spot); and predict what might happen next (*Each Peach Pear Plum* (Ahlberg 1977), *Handa's Surprise* (Browne 1994)).

Second, picture books start the literary habit of helping readers to make connections between books and life. We see this as children and toddlers point to objects they recognize in a book, or even go off and bring the object to the book if possible (Miffy's drinking mug, Spot's school bag, an avocado pear). Many picture book authors/illustrators go even further by creating characters who munch real holes in the book (e.g. *The Very Hungry Caterpillar* (Carle 1970)), or play 'peepo' through actual spy-holes in the pages (e.g. *Peepo* (Ahlberg 1981)), and even tell us that they have accidentally got stuck in the book (*The Little Mouse Trapped in a Book* (Felix 1975)). What all this is doing for babies and early years readers is involving them in a book world so that they bring their experiences to it, but also teaching them how to borrow the book's characters and events to add to their own store of explanations for things that happen ('Paddington's got red wellies like mine'; 'our cat eats six dinners'; 'the snowman sat in a freezer like ours').

Third, all these experiences with picture books teach most of the basic literary conventions: beginnings and ways-in to narrative; plot complications, problems and challenges; the resolving of difficulties; and happy endings. We know this has been effective when young children begin to use these literary devices in their own oral stories and early writing.

Finally, and most obviously, picture books have small and manageable examples of print so that young emerging readers are gradually introduced to the notion that the black marks carry meanings, as do the pictures. Furthermore, small chunks of print (words) can be examined carefully and they gradually become associated with the repeated appearances of favourite characters. As young readers notice individual letters they are often linked with the increasingly familiar letters in their own names, or the names of brothers and sisters ('I begin like Nellie the elephant' [Natalie]). Picture books play a complex and significant part in introducing children to literature and preparing them for literacy.

Supporting young listeners and tellers

Encouraging young children to tell their own stories and listen to the stories we can tell them and read to them is the most significant contribution we can make to ensuring that they become not just efficiently literate, but passionately hooked on books and keen to write. We now know that it is never too soon to begin sharing books with our babies and we can take advantage of the fact that libraries are at last eager to welcome baby and toddler borrowers. Supermarkets are also making big efforts to stock a range of good quality books for young children in low cost paperback form. But even if we cannot afford to buy books we probably have wonderful collections of old rhymes, tongue-twisters, songs, and finger and toe rhymes (e.g. This little piggy went to market; Tommy thumb; Ten little squirrels) locked away in our memories. Or, if we really have no remembered folk material from our cultural inheritance to share, we can get help from older people and other community leaders, or community bookshops, social clubs, child welfare clinics and libraries.

This social and community approach to helping our babies and young children begin the journey to literacy is far better than waiting for schools to do it all. In fact, without the active help and involvement of carers and communities, schools cannot succeed in teaching literacy to all our children. There is a great danger in believing that there are easy short cuts to literacy which can be ordered by government and simply carried out by teachers. Literacy is a complex achievement with roots deep in the earliest days of infancy and all carers, families and early years professionals are teachers of literacy as they sing nursery rhymes, rock babies to sleep with old songs, tell stories about their own childhoods, listen to toddlers' tales of monsters under the bed and share picture books.

Provision and activities

- People. See the suggestions under this heading at the end of Chapter 2.
- Places. See the suggestions under this heading at the end of Chapters 1 and 2.

- Things to do.   All the suggestions under this heading at the end of Chapters 1 and 2 are relevant because literacy and language development go hand in hand.

This chapter has given detailed guidance on how to approach storytelling, but some comments on sharing a book with a baby and some suggestions for books to use with young children follow.

Sharing a book with a baby

Choose moments when the baby is alert and you are not distracted by other people or jobs to do. Make yourself and the baby comfortable (a personal choice this – sitting on the floor, on cushions, on a bed or in a comfy chair) and choose a book which is easy to hold near the baby's focus (probably only a few inches) and reach (touching pages and pictures is to be encouraged). The choice of book should be decided by such matters as your enjoyment of the story or rhyme, your pleasure in singing and rocking with the rhythms of the language, your pleasure in the words (if any), and how much you like the illustrations and are able to make up stories about them. For the baby's sake you must be prepared to repeat the same books many times and start with a small collection, which can become familiar and well loved, before adding new books. Try to keep the baby's books together in a special place, preferably low down and accessible for a toddler once the crawling and walking stages are reached. At first, book sessions with a baby will be brief and depend on how long the baby is focused on the activity, but the opportunity can also be extended by singing and dancing with the baby or playing music.

Some book suggestions

Folk-fairy tales
The Puffin Baby and Toddler Treasury (Viking 1998).
Tales of Wonder and Magic by Berlie Doherty (Walker Books 1997).
Favourite Fairy Tales by Sarah Hayes (Walker Books 1997).
Flossie and the Fox by Patricia McKissak (Puffin 1986).
The Story of Chicken Licken by Jan Ormerod (Walker Books 1985).
The Goose that Laid the Golden Egg by Geoffrey Patterson (Picture Piper 1986).
The Illustrated Book of Fairy Tales retold by Neil Philip (Dorling Kindersley 1997).
Hansel and Gretel by Jane Ray (Walker Books 1997).

Goldilocks and the Three Bears by Tony Ross (Andersen 1976).
The Three Little Wolves and the Big Bad Pig by Eugene Trivizas (Heinemann 1993).

Myths and legends
The Mousehole Cat by Antonia Barber (Walker Books 1990).
Seasons of Splendour by Madhur Jaffrey (Puffin 1985).
Creation Stories from Around the World by Ann Pilling (Walker Books 1997).
Mufaro's Beautiful Daughters by John Steptoe (Hodder & Stoughton 1987).

Nursery rhymes and poetry
Bringing the Rain to Kapiti Plain by Verna Aardema (Macmillan 1981).
I Din Do Nuttin by John Agard (Bodley 1983).
A Caribbean Dozen by John Agard and Grace Nichols (Walker Books 1994).
Each Peach Pear Plum by Janet and Allan Ahlberg (Picture Lions 1977).
This Little Puffin by Elizabeth Matterson (Puffin 1969).
My Very First Mother Goose by Iona Opie (Walker Books 1996).
We're Going on a Bear Hunt by Michael Rosen (Walker Books 1989).
Hairy Tales and Nursery Crimes by Michael Rosen (Young Lions 1985).
Don't Put Mustard in the Custard by Michael Rosen (Puffin 1985).
The Cat in the Hat by Dr Seuss (Harper Collins 1957).
A Child's Garden of Verses by Robert Louis Stevenson (Gollancz 1997, first published 1885)

Picture books
Ten, Nine, Eight by Molly Bang (Puffin 1983).
My Brother Sean by Petronella Breinburg (Puffin 1973).
The Bear by Raymond Briggs (Red Fox 1994).
Willy the Dreamer by Anthony Browne (Walker Books 1997).
Granpa by John Burningham (Puffin 1984).
Jasper's Beanstalk by Nick Butterworth (Hodder & Stoughton 1992).
Little Monster Did It by Helen Cooper (Picture Corgi 1995).
The Bear Under the Stairs by Helen Cooper (Picture Corgi 1993).
The Little Mouse Trapped in a Book by Monique Felix (Methuen 1975).
Alfie Gets in First by Shirley Hughes (Picture Lions 1981).
Rosie's Walk by Pat Hutchins (Puffin 1968).
Nothing by Mick Inkpen (Hodder & Stoughton, Knight 1995).
Bear by Mick Inkpen (Hodder & Stoughton, Knight 1997).
Two Bears and Joe by Penelope Lively (Viking 1995).
Not Now, Bernard by David McKee (Arrow 1980).
Five Minutes Peace by Jill Murphy (Walker Books 1986).
Where The Wild Things Are by Maurice Sendak (Puffin 1967).
Can't You Sleep Little Bear? by Martin Waddell (Walker Books 1988).

Farmer Duck by Martin Waddell (Walker Books 1991).
John Brown, Rose and the Midnight Cat by Jenny Wagner (Puffin 1977).

Alphabet books
Quentin Blake's ABC by Quentin Blake (Jonathan Cape 1989).
What's Inside? The Alphabet Book by Satoshi Kitamura (A&C Black 1985).
I Spy: An Alphabet in Art by Lucy Micklethwait (Collins 1992).
The Bad Day ABC by Hilda Offen (Hamish Hamilton 1997).
Michael Rosen's ABC by Michael Rosen (Macdonald Young Books 1996).
Dr Seuss's ABC by Dr Seuss (Collins 1963).
F-Freezing ABC by Posy Simmonds (Jonathan Cape 1995).

Further reading

Butler, D. (1979) *Cushla and Her Books*. Sevenoaks: Hodder & Stoughton.
Engel, S. (1995) *The Stories Children Tell: Making Sense of the Narratives of Childhood*. New York: W. H. Freeman.
Fox, C. (1993) *At the Very Edge of the Forest: The Influence of Literature on Storytelling by Children*. London: Cassell.
Rosen, B. (1991) *Shapers and Polishers: Teachers as Storytellers*. London: Mary Glasgow.

4

Literacy begins here

> As I sounded the words 'cheep 'cheep' in one story for example Cecilia
> (3-4) remarked, that's like 'cheese' and as the word 'supper' in the
> story of *John Brown, Rose and the Midnight Cat* was read she observed
> 'That's like shopping 'cos it's got two 'p's. A further example revealed
> the actual word scanning process in operation even though it was a
> short word. Cecilia (3-3) identified the word 'zoo' and remarked
> 'That's got two 'o's and a zebra'.
>
> (Payton 1984: 80)

Three-year-old Cecilia's confident and highly personal ability to recognize
the sounds and letters of words in her favourite books indicates that literacy begins early and is rooted in the kinds of experiences with people, languages and print described in the previous three chapters. In just over three
years a child may move from her first gasping cries at birth to Cecilia's bril-
liant word recognition and analysis of 'two "o"s and a zebra'. This remarkable journey begins with the baby's desire to communicate, as outlined in
Chapter 1, and is all about making and sharing meanings with carers and
others. The possibilities of playing with language, sounds and meanings
add some interesting features to early language learning (see Chapter 2)
and the child's literacy journey gets more exciting as the possibilities of
stories and narrative reveal a new landscape (see Chapter 3). So, many more
ways of making sense of our experiences are available in stories and books,
including opportunities for exploring personal identity and our links with

family groups and cultures. Stories also fortify us – adults as much as children – against anxiety, loss and the many disasters and mishaps of life. The remarkable way in which literacy, or the writing system of a culture, continues and expands these possibilities and accelerates the wonderful start many young children have made as communicators, meaning-makers, linguists and storytellers will be the subject of this chapter.

Representation

Literacy certainly gets started long before most parents and carers recognize it and the widely accepted academic view is that literacy begins with the thinking processes and activities known broadly as *representation*. This is a rather daunting theory but we can turn to Cecilia for a little help and guidance as we explore it. In the passage quoted above she describes the letter 'z' in 'zoo' as 'zebra', and we can assume that her most vivid and frequent encounters with the letter 'z' have been as the initial letter of 'zebra'. Many young children are excited and attracted by pictures (in books and on television) of the dramatically black-and-white striped horse-like zebra, often accompanied by its word label, and for English speakers and readers the rarely occurring initial letter 'z' is a highly memorable letter shape. For Cecilia, 'zebra' actually represents 'z' – it is a visual, emotional and written symbol which packs a special kind of punch for her whenever she meets it. Symbols work like this for all of us – they are a focus for our feelings and stand for, or represent, whole ranges of emotions, thoughts, experiences and cultural traditions (just think how often British children see zebras in alphabet books and friezes, and in animal and zoo books). Such symbolic representations actually help us to think, whatever our age, because they provide ready-made summaries of complicated events and experiences. Children also make marks and drawings which are their personal symbolic representations or summaries at a very early age and families and early childhood settings often display these pictures of 'mum', 'a tree', 'a lorry', etc. Representations help children and adults to hold on to, or recall, things and people in their absence (e.g. a zebra seen previously in a picture alphabet book), and to make new connections between similar images, objects, events and marks (e.g. this word 'zoo' starts like my special favourite 'zebra').

Representations have been described as a huge family of activities (Matthews 1994) and also include such important forms of early childhood thinking and action as talk, play, stories, mime, dance, model making and building, mark making, painting, drawing and writing. Young children participate in all these activities and use them as ways of representing or thinking through their experiences of – and present knowledge about – people, emotions, life and the entire universe! Many observations of children's representational thinking can be found in the previous chapters – for example, the play repertoire of the little girl on the tube train. Now we have to add to this family of representational thinking activities the processes of early writing and reading, but a word of warning about the 'special' nature of literacy may be useful at this point.

Warning!

Although the process of representational thinking (including early mark making) may be a natural and distinctive feature of our species (like verbal language), literacy is a latecomer in human history and is a cultural invention of human groups. Some highly complex societies in the past did not evolve writing systems and it is a fairly modern idea to expect all the individuals in a society to read and write competently. The universal ability to read and write is a measure of social, educational and economic progress in modern nations, while for individuals being literate makes all the difference to their chances of social acceptability, worthwhile employment, extended educational opportunities and material success. These hugely important issues explain not just the power of literacy but the pain and the pressure it puts on young children and their families and communities. Knowing the terrible handicaps of illiteracy in our society and desperate to see our own children reading and writing we may, with the best of intentions, adopt approaches and practices which make reading and writing narrow and pointless. This will undermine our children's true literacy interests and strategies. However, this is not a 'lay off teaching' warning, but a 'trust and observe young learners so that you know what help and information to give' plea, and it underpins the entire philosophy of this book.

The discussion of children's literacy development which follows will begin with 'writing' because, contrary to many assumptions, children's early writing often starts long before reading, although looking at books and listening to stories feed into early writing attempts and accelerate the development of early understanding of the alphabet and spelling.

Making marks

Very young children begin to make marks as they smear their spilt food across a table or wall, drag their fingers through pools of liquid, use a lipstick on a mirror, scribble over the print in books and magazines, or even get to grips with the paper, paint, pens and crayons adults prefer them to use. There is also growing evidence that very young children who have access to computer word-processing and paint programs make similar marks and drawings (Kent 1997). It is all too easy to dismiss these marks as 'scribbles' and 'mess' and of no significance, yet a moment's thought should convince us that exciting things are happening. For a start, these young children are making their mark in the world and this is a metaphor we frequently use to praise someone's achievements, although it originates in the days when illiterate adults could only sign documents by 'making their mark' (usually a cross). More importantly, children's early mark-making activities have three major characteristics which are usually associated with literacy: creativity, communication and some degree of permanence.

Creativity

The idea that early marks are creative is not an exaggeration because even a sticky chocolate smear on a wall or tablecloth is new in the world, the trace of an action and evidence of the existence of the child who made the mark. These first marks may begin as 'accidents' but they stay long enough to be noticed, commented on and even repeated on other occasions and with other tools (because chocolate on walls does not always get the praise that early mark making deserves!). A long process of creative mark making is triggered by these first happy accidents with food, dribbles, damp surfaces and the more conventional materials used for writing in homes and care settings. Researchers suggest that first mark making is triggered by an inner developmental programme (Matthews 1994), rather like verbal language and walking, and that these early marks are representations of movement, space, shape and emotions. In simple terms, very young children are making a movement with a marker for the pleasurable physical sensations it gives, or exploring shape and space as they experience them, and also working through varied feelings and emotional responses. If all these things occur while markers and surfaces of some kind are to hand then a permanent representation (or mark/picture) of the experience is made. Is this so very different from all the art forms which human groups have developed over the centuries?

Communication

The marks made by young children certainly communicate the fact that the young mark makers exist, but children soon begin to use their own marks as 'signs' which carry messages. So they start to give their marks names or labels – e.g. 'a lorry', 'a worm' – in a similar fashion to the way older children and adults 'recognize' the shapes of faces and animals in cloud formations. As children's marks become more like drawings – or representations of generally recognizable objects – the young artists will explain them with story-like captions: 'All the people in the house' (Payton 1984: 38). This is a very common example of a child making sense of experience and using his or her own representations as a powerful kind of thinking and communication. So strong is the young child's drive to understand all kinds of representations and make sense of them that she or he will even 'humanize' geometrical shapes (see Figure 4.1). This draw- ing is by a 4-year-old (4 years 3 months) Chinese girl in a London primary school nursery class who was given some plastic logi-blocks to draw round, but then found her own way of making human sense of the task.

Permanence

Marks, like writing and print, are permanent in that they exist long enough for us to think about them and/or save them for others to see and

Figure 4.1　A child has made a drawing from the outlines of plastic geometric shapes.

share. Marks and writing can be destroyed and there is certainly a place in all good literacy learning and teaching for waste-paper bins, recycle bins and shredders, but writing and early marks can also be corrected, changed and improved. Very young children's mark-making changes as it is influenced by the print they encounter in their immediate environments and by the enthusiasm of adults who recognize and praise these attempts at writing. Even the scribble patterns of young children begin to look like the flowing lines of 'real writing' and collections of apparently random marks – as well as drawings and paintings – start to include recognizable letters and numerals.

The desire to communicate and create permanent messages leads many young children to put marks on family shopping lists, answer pads, notes and letters, or write their own versions of their names on books, magazines, drawings and scraps of paper. These developments are at the heart of literacy because the young communicators are 'joining the literacy club' (Smith 1988) of their culture by creating messages ('"Mummy, this says someone's crying, someone's singing, someone's playing Lord Kumba Ya" (Cecilia 3-8)' (Payton 1984: 45)) and receiving the messages of others ('"Where it say 'toot'?" (Cecilia 3-3)' (Payton 1984: 68)). During these early stages in the literacy process children already experience something of the organizing power and emotional impact of the written system. They make lists and inventories of names and logos they know (people, pets, shops, foods or even storybook characters – see Figure 4.2), or use their names as markers of ownership on books, toys and doors, or as signs of love and affection on scraps of paper given as presents to special friends and carers. But at this point the nature of mark making is changing as young children begin to investigate print closely and find out about its relationships to the sounds of their languages.

Writing sounds

It is helpful to think of young children's early writing as a response to an exciting literacy problem: how do you break into the system which encodes (puts into written/graphic symbols) the sounds and meanings of spoken language so that you can be a full member of 'the literacy club'? The first step in tackling this problem is to ask the right questions and get help from those 'in the know'. The sooner this happens the better, as the studies of sharing books with babies are indicating, and it is clear that young children find little difficulty in asking the right questions if certain optimum conditions are maintained. The nature and pacing of the help given by carers and educators requires sensitivity and insight of the sort

Figure 4.2   The names of storybook characters.

which comes from close and caring involvement with young children and a desire to learn more about them.

The right questions

The right questions can be summarized as:

- What does that say?
- How do you write . . .?

How often have we all half-heard these questions from a young child and not realized how significant they are to literacy development? With these two broad questions about print, young children are hypothesizing or creating theories about how the entire system works. The answers we give must be as prompt and as well-tuned as possible to the child's requirements and as simply honest and true as we can make them. These major questions about literacy are huge achievements in themselves and reflect some very sophisticated thinking by young children about the nature of communication, spoken language, print and representing sounds by grouping graphic signs in regular patterns. These are complex ideas for all of us and they cannot readily be simplified but we do not have to launch into complicated explanations in response to our children's literacy questions. We just have to behave like enthusiastic and helpful writers and readers ourselves and tell our children what the print 'says' and show them how to write their own words and messages.

For example, during meals or at the shops we can read the words and the instructions on the packets and wrappers of familiar foods: 'That word is "Sugarpops", see the "S" it starts with? What else do you like to eat that starts with "S"? . . . Smarties - that's right! Shall we write Smarties on our shopping list for this afternoon?'

Of course this is a slightly exaggerated example and not all these questions need to be asked at any one time, but it does illustrate the opportunities for investigating and learning about literacy in the homeliest of situations.

Optimum conditions

The responses we make to children's questions about print will demonstrate some of the ways in which sounds are written, but even to get to first base in literacy does require some optimum conditions. Clearly children cannot ask the right questions about print if they do not encounter enough of it to rouse their curiosity, nor will they risk the questions and make 'good guesses' if the whole business appears to be threatening and creates anxiety. However, we can create the optimum literacy conditions for young children in remarkably simple ways and the following slogans may be helpful indicators:

- print should be for real;
- print should be for pleasure;
- print should be for proper investigation.

Print for real

Print for real is no problem in the contemporary world which swamps us with printed matter, and although swamping young children is not intended here, the everyday kind of print we find in our homes, streets, shops and clubs, and on our clothes, televisions and computers is particularly useful. It is genuine print about real things that matter to people and it is easily found, played with and thrown away when it gets tatty. It is often associated with good motivating experiences such as: visits to fast-food restaurants; trips on buses and trains; gifts on special occasions; letters from relatives; visits to places of worship; pretending to be a grown-up filling in forms in the bank or post office; and favourite cereals and yogurts collected from the supermarket shelf. All you need is bags of everyday print and, if possible, access to a qwerty keyboard or computer word-processing program (see Kent 1997). There is no necessity to buy special early writing and reading exercise books or expensive software which promises to teach 'pre-school children' all about the alphabet, phonics and spelling. These materials will not allow the children to ask their own questions about print and invent their own experimental systems for writing, and they may instil a belief that there is only one right answer to every question and wrong answers must be avoided.

Print for pleasure

Print should be for pleasure and we must provide young children with ample opportunities to play and muck about with the system – hence the importance of collecting and using cheap and meaningful materials. The atmosphere in which we play at being readers and writers with our children must also be relaxed and open-ended so that they feel able to take risks and exploit words, sounds and graphic symbols. Chapter 2 is of direct relevance here and it is at this point that we need to be sure our children encounter songs, chants, rhymes, tongue-twisters, poetry and rhythmic dances and games every day.

Print for investigation

Print should be available for close investigation because children learn in ways which are very like the behaviour of serious scientists: they observe closely, hypothesize or tell a possible story about what they have noticed, and then try out this theory on the material or event that has interested them. If this does not give an acceptable explanation they try to change the parts of their theory that appear to be adrift. An example of this approach to spoken language and word meanings was given in Chapter 2 when my grandson Daniel had to revise his hypothesis about my use of the word 'ornamental' in referring to some ducks. When it comes to investigating print a young child may see the name of a supermarket chain which starts with 'S' and announce 'That says my name – Sanjay'. The child does not believe that he is called 'Sainsbury' but he is aware of the significance of initial letters and the sound that is common to the beginning of his name and that of the grocery store. My granddaughter developed an early fascination with initial letters and created her own alphabets as well as using initial letters to label the figures in her many drawings of kings, queens, princesses and beautiful ladies (see Figure 4.3). Here we have evidence of an early start to finding out about English spelling patterns by a 4-year-old bilingual child. Her interest was stimulated by wide exposure to at least three languages and lots of different alphabets – in books, on posters and friezes – and by having fun making lists of people, places, foods, animals, etc. which start with the same sounds.

Young writers' strategies

Young children have their own strategies for finding out more about how to write sounds and when these are supported by caring and knowledgeable adults they take the children a long way towards understanding the system. I have written about these strategies before (Whitehead 1996) and will only outline them briefly here.

Asking questions

Children ask us directly about what print means and how to write it.

Figure 4.3   Initial letters on drawings by a 4-year-old.

Watching others

Children watch other people writing and try to do it themselves, especially when their 'models' are loved and admired. So, they do a shopping list alongside mum, even imitating her sighs, pencil sucking and crossing out of items.

Using names

Children's names are full of significance as signs that they exist and have a place in the world, but they are also a very familiar example of a set of sound and symbol combinations which give some clues about how the system works. This means not just initial letters but terminal (end) patterns like 'er' or 'ia' and combinations such as 'ch' and 'st'.

Exploiting knowledge

Even if they only know their own name, or a few letters of it, children will use this ingeniously to create a message. For example, my 3-year-old granddaughter would write letters to me consisting of her name at the top of the paper and the rest of the sheet filled with rows of kisses and letter-like marks. Another child wrote to tell me it was her fourth birthday by filling a page with her name repeated in neat rows and putting a row of 4s (often seen on birthday cakes and cards in her nursery centre) at the bottom of the sheet. These children were using what written signs they did know and having a pretend go at the unknown bits, but they were definitely communicating important human messages.

Using alphabets and sounds

Young children delight in alphabets and soon recognize initial letters and their sounds; this ties in with their delight in playing with language sounds, rhymes and nonsense. This can lead to the gradual realization that the continuous stream of spoken language must be broken down into separate words and groups of sounds. Many children use the names of letters to create a semi-phonetic code for writing: RUDF = are you deaf? (Bissex 1980: 3). Or they write only the easily heard consonants: TBL = table, NMBR = number.

Some milestones in early writing

There are patterns to young children's development as writers and we need to be sensitive to these and able to keep observations and records of the milestones. This is particularly important because these develop-mental processes of literacy are not always valued by conventional approaches to teaching children to write, which concentrate on copying and practising letter formation. However, some valuable guidelines do exist. For instance, the remarkable provision and philosophy in the Reggio Emilia kindergartens of Italy where children are enabled to move from 'gifts of communication' – exchanging objects, messages, words and skills via loans and borrowings – to written messages and love letters, because every child has a personal mail box (Reggio Emilia 1996). A British approach to assessing young children's writing (Gorman and Brooks 1996) provides a useful outline of stages to look for, beginning with 'drawing and sign writing' and moving through 'letter-like forms', 'copied letters', 'child's name and strings of letters', 'words', 'sentences' and 'text'. (And ending with 'a bit of theory' for parents and teachers.)

The milestones which follow are based on my own research over a number of years in several London nursery schools and classes and may help you to notice and record the writing development of the young chil-dren in your care. They will also help you to understand the achievements of the young children in the case studies in the next chapter.

Scribble

This is an important breakthrough as it indicates the child's awareness that 'writing' is not the same as pictures and drawing. Scribble is spiky and often in lines (linear) and even written with the speed and flourish of 'real' writers. (We may need to be wary when we use the word 'scribble' to describe children's writing because many adults use the word to indicate meaningless rubbish!)

Isolated letters and numerals

Both conventional and invented letters and numerals appear in ones, twos or more, scattered among drawings, paintings and lines of scribble. This is evidence of the impact of the conventional written systems the child is exposed to in its home, group setting and community, and of the child's growing interest in them.

Lists and inventories

These appear as well-organized listings in horizontal and vertical lines of individual conventional letters and numerals, and invented letter-like forms. A later development will sometimes appear as standard lists of names (friends, family, food, storybook and television characters). These seem to be personal checklists of what the child knows and can write unaided, and also enable the child to create satisfying chunks of text. Later lists may be a way of thinking about and organizing information.

Own name

As discussed above, personal names give children clues about how written language represents the sound system of the spoken language and they are immensely important as badges of identity and ownership. Children can discover written conventions like double consonants (Dennis), alternative spellings and variants (Ann, Anne, Anna) and different languages (Jamila, Yvette, Sian). Children are often very determined to 'get it right' when writing their own names and will self-correct and persevere at the task for long periods. The first isolated letters we find in children's drawings and mark making are often those from their own names.

Words and pictures

An exciting early development in young children's literacy is the occurrence of pictures accompanied by written captions. These may appear as lines of scribble, collections (strings) of conventional letters, 'words' labelling figures and objects in the drawing, and readable semi-phonetic bits of text. The importance of this milestone is that it once again indicates an understanding of the differences between drawing and writing, but it is also a very significant indicator of the power and influence of books on the child's thinking. The child is beginning to investigate a striking feature of literate and bookish cultures – i.e. that pictures and words together tell stories and complement each other.

Phonological awareness and spelling

This is the point at which many children find the courage to trust what they hear and have a go at representing it using letters and groups of letters whose 'sounds' they know. The resulting invented spellings tell us what children understand about written and spoken language and what they are trying to work out next. In order to break into conventional spelling young children have to take risks and this means that they must have a strong desire to communicate and be confident that the readers of their communications will respond to the messages appropriately. Some of the most delightful examples of this kind of writing are private notes, letters and complaints: 'I HIVANT HAD A TR IN PAD' (I haven't had a turn in Playdough) (Newkirk 1984: 341). Clearly the problem of democratic and fair access to the Playdough must be sorted out and this 4-year-old should be praised for her excellent grasp of the sounds of American English and their alphabetic representation, before she is encouraged to look at some of the complex patterns of standardized spelling.

Finally, it is important to remember that these are just some milestones which I have noticed and found interesting. They are not rigid stages through which all children should pass and many children do miss out many of them, or pass through them rapidly or when we are not looking. Other people's milestones are only useful if they encourage you to start collecting your own examples of children's marks, drawings and writing, and begin mapping out milestones for the children you know, care for and educate.

Reading for meaning

Many settings are too concerned that children can recognize certain words, so that 'barking at print' becomes the core of the 'hearing children read' session. What adults *should* be encouraging is reading for meaning. This begins with all the important story and narrative activities described in the previous chapter and it is clearly the most important reason for sharing books with babies. In fact, reading for meaning is the foundation of all literacy and any definition of 'reading' that does not have the communication of meaning at its centre is nonsensical. Reading without gaining, or at least searching for, meaning is just performing tricks with print and no more significant than a parrot's mimicry of words. Meaningful reading starts with *shared approaches* in which children and adults are partners; it involves learning to *ask questions of texts* (print and pictures); and it requires that the beginner reader is able to *predict likely outcomes*.

Shared approaches

Early reading is most successful when children and adults share the pleasures of looking at books, reading them together and talking about them on many occasions. These literary experiences are created by adult-child literacy partnerships in which the older and wiser partner starts by taking on a great deal of the reading and at first leads the discussion about what the text is about. However, this should never leave the child with nothing to do as even a very young child can be helped to focus on the book, point at a picture, bounce up and down to the repeated and rhythmic language patterns or repeat crucial names and phrases from the text (see Chapter 3).

Older and more experienced infant readers will know favourite books word for word, be able to read along with the adult, and be able to take over the reading of favourite passages and repeated rhymes and phrases. If wordless picture books or books with very few words are shared, the child can be encouraged to take on much greater responsibility for creating a narrative which is guided by the pictures.

It is worth emphasizing at this point that children who know the words or story of a book 'off by heart' or who use the pictures as cues to re-create the narrative line are doing something which is very skilled and essential to competent reading when they start going it alone. If young children know the words of a book from memory they actually have a pattern or model of the story in their heads which they can then match to the pages of the book (the text). Any mismatches which occur as they try to read and then find that they 'run out of ' words or pages, or have 'too many left over', will actually help them to focus more closely on the text and on the appearance and patterns of groups of words and individual words. Similarly, the 'reading' of pictures is a sophisticated skill and one at which young children born and brought up with television, video and computer icons soon excel. Such an apparently obvious matter as recognizing similar images of a main character on page after page is a sophisticated literary convention which is gradually understood by young children as they investigate whether there are lots of Little Bears, or just the same Little Bear who can't get to sleep? An artist's use of horizontal lines, flying clothes and bending trees and grass to indicate running and speed are not 'natural' and must be learnt by lots of book sharing and discussions about passages like this: *'Jemima Puddle-Duck was not much in the habit of flying. She ran downhill a few yards flapping her shawl, and then she jumped off into the air'* (Potter [1908] 1989: 163).

Shared partnerships with books bring another bonus: they help children to literally see and hear print being brought to life by a familiar voice. The child can watch the text, hear the words and identify the meanings partly because the human voice can express so much meaning. This is a very important reading lesson for young children who are sitting close to caring adults, seeing the print symbols and hearing the related sounds, whether of wonderful nonsense words like 'Rumpeta, Rumpeta' from *The Elephant and the Bad Baby* (Vipont 1969), or familiar phrases such as *'Eat up Gemma'* (Hayes 1988).

Questioning the text

Successful readers learn to ask questions of any text they meet in order to search out its meanings and, just as importantly, its relevance for them. We all scan reading matter in this way – from personal letters and public notices to novels, poems and newspaper stories. Furthermore, successful readers bring their own questions to a text and this is particularly obvious when the text is a reference book or a handbook for some new equipment (How do you 'save' on this computer? Will the microwave defrost a cream cake? Where is Patagonia?). But good readers also bring their own 'life and death' questions to the reading of novels, biographies, history, poetry and even television and radio 'soaps'.

Young children make a very early start on these big questions about the human condition and they are always wanting to know 'who loves me?', 'why do some children not like me?' and 'why do people go away?'. Stories, books, plays and television and radio 'soaps' give children (and adults) the chance to verbalize these difficult questions safely by focusing them on fictional characters and imaginary situations. All that is required for the young child to do this is a reading partner who encourages careful examination of pictures and print, rereads texts many times and creates opportunities for lots of talk about favourite stories, pictures and characters.

The research literature is full of examples of very young readers who are concerned about motives – 'She's nice ain't she? [referring to the beautiful wicked queen in Snow White]' (Payton 1984: 56); emotions – 'Cushla solicitously kissed his howling little face at every reading . . . Her identification with Sean was complete' (Butler 1979: 50); and the unstated aspects of story plots 'Did Rosie know that the fox was following her?' (Hutchins 1968).

Predicting likely outcomes

It is a short step from asking questions of texts to making predictions about what is likely to happen and this is one of the crucial skills for the experienced reader as well as for the young beginner. The ability fluent readers have to pick up meaning at great speed and process lengthy and complex texts without losing their way is rooted in their fast and ever-changing predictions about texts at several levels, including overall meaning, individual word meanings, instant word recognition, letter-sound combinations, print conventions and cultural expectations to name a few! This may be complex but it has to start somewhere and very early encounters between books, babies and adults seem once again to be at the heart of literacy.

Many modern picture books make it particularly easy and enjoyable to predict the outcomes of a situation and talk about life and relationships. One very striking example is the interruption of the printed story line by a series of full page pictures without captions in the middle of *Where the*

Wild Things Are (Sendak 1967). This picture sequence occurs at the main pivot of the narrative, a kind of big decision time for Max – will he stay as king of the Wild Things or return home? The young reader is in effect required to participate actively in making this difficult decision as she or he is drawn into pages of wild rumpus through dream-like jungles with smiling monsters who are remarkably obedient to a small boy in a sleep-suit and a gold crown.

Many picture books use large picture spreads to draw the young reader into thinking about and predicting appropriate moves for fictional characters. Even an Old English Sheepdog can raise some of the most difficult emotional issues in *John Brown, Rose and the Midnight Cat* (Wagner 1977) when he is depicted thinking about his jealous reaction to a stray cat. Over several pages of stunning artwork the reader must agonize with this tormented creature and debate the pros and cons of love, loneliness, old age, jealousy and forgiveness.

All this may seem to be strong stuff for small children but books intended for them are as rich in hilarious decisions – will anyone ever buy a dog called *'Arthur'* (Graham 1984) who is trying to look like any animal pet except a dog? – as they are in narrow escapes from disasters like locking yourself inside the house, as in *Alfie Gets in First* (Hutchins 1981). It seems that young readers can manage all these challenging predictions if they have a reading partner who helps them to scan pictures closely by talking about them and focusing their attention on certain details: 'Where is Alfie going now? What is he carrying?'; 'What is John Brown thinking about?'; 'Would *you* like to stay with the Wild Things?'. Similar queries can be voiced as we discuss the plot of a favourite book and speculate about what will be left in Handa's basket (Browne 1994), or where Spot (Hill 1980) might hide in our house, nursery or playgroup.

Of course this must all be done gently, over time and with many enthusiastic rereadings, but what these features of reading for meaning in the early years do is help children to become active readers. The absolutely essential reading lesson we are sharing with young children at this stage is that reading is an active, searching, thinking, meaning-making and hugely enjoyable experience.

Close encounters with words

Cecilia Payton was looking closely at print before she was three and other babies have been fascinated by the print on calendars and the bold graphics of Dick Bruna's *Miffy* books (Butler 1979). Modern research is still full of observations of young children who learn to love print as much as pictures and understand that it carries messages (Hall 1987; Scrivens 1995; Campbell 1996; Miller 1996). This should give us the confidence to try and stimulate our children's close encounters with print by developing some enjoyable strategies for sharing books and reading print of all kinds. Three helpful strategies for focusing closely on words with a young child are: behaving like *word detectives*, lots of *alphabet play* and noticing and playing with *similar sounds*.

Word detectives

Adult encouragement of an investigative and playful approach to close encounters with words helps young children to be active word detectives as they scan print. The aim is to support children so that they develop problem-solving attitudes to all aspects of literacy, search for clues to word identity and meaning and notice regular letter and sound patterns which can be predicted. As children grow in confidence and experience they are able to bring all their earlier literacy and life experiences to bear on words and texts, but in the early days they need to borrow the experience and skill of an older reading partner. In close one-to-one or small-group book sharing situations very young children can be shown important words such as characters' names (these often appear in the titles of books and are printed boldly on book covers), place names and authors' and illustrators' names. They can also be shown those powerful words in a text which carry emotional information such as 'love', 'angry', 'kiss', 'happy' and 'cry'. Sometimes special graphic effects are used for these words and others, like 'crash', 'ouch', 'buzz' and 'no' – just like the print effects in comics ('boom', 'splat', 'pow'). All these ways of drawing attention to print and the con- ventions of spelling develop alphabetic and phonological awareness in exciting and meaningful ways. Furthermore, repeated words which carry lots of meaning and emotional power can soon be recognized by very young readers and they can first join in with saying them and then be encouraged to say them alone while the adult reader stays silent. This applies as much to road names, advertising hoardings and notices in the supermarket as to favourite books. It is a bit like the practice of leaving gaps in early conversations with babies so that they can slot in their gurgles and word approximations.

Alphabet play

Children do need to develop alphabetic awareness so that they can recog- nize letters of the alphabet, know their names and make a start on associ- ating them with some of their commoner sounds. We must not be too rigid about the sounds individual letters make as these vary in English and are greatly changed by the letters they are grouped with in words and by certain historical aspects of the development of standardized English spellings. We must always refer to the sounds of individual letters or letter strings in meaningful and enjoyable words, texts and stories.

There are lots of opportunities for alphabet play in traditional songs and rhymes: A was an archer who shot at a frog; Great A, little a, Bouncing B, The cat's in the cupboard and she can't see me; Pat-cake, pat-a-cake, baker's man. Or in the nonsense alphabets of Edward Lear (R was a rabbit Who had a bad habit Of eating the flowers In gardens and bowers), and the beautiful modern alphabet books, posters and friezes widely available in shops, libraries and early years settings.

Play with alphabets, common letter sounds and alphabetic order can be encouraged if children make their own lists of 'things that begin with A' etc. and move on to building up their own alphabets of things, people, places and experiences that matter to them. Of course these activities should also involve lots of drawing, cutting and sticking, or using a computer or typewriter keyboard – as the children see fit, and depending on resources. Lots of opportunities to look at and play with address books, telephone directories, A to Z street directories, first dictionaries and word books can stimulate interest in alphabets and give young children useful insights into the ways in which letters – singly and in groups – represent the sounds of the language.

Similar sounds

Developing young children's sensitivity to the sounds of language – the same, the similar, the near-echoes and all sorts of variations – can best be done by surrounding them with poetry, rhyme and verse. From this jumping-off point we can begin to alert them in their close encounters with words to the fact that similar sounds will show up as similar spelling patterns. Of course we would be unwise to put it to them as baldly as that – we need to play the word detectives game so that they see words which start with the same letters and hear how similar they sound. This is of course the poetic device of alliteration and also relates to young children's interest in initial letters. Sensitivity to initial letters in words comes early and can often be increased by learning alliterative tongue-twisters and traditional nursery rhymes (e.g. Davy Davy Dumpling, Boil him in a pot), or noticing some advertising slogans. The same and similar endings of words are soon heard by children who have a rich store of songs and poetry to draw on, because this is the aspect of language sound which we call rhyme. When looking at print with children we can point out the rhymes and draw attention to the fact that words have endings as well as beginnings:

> Dance to your daddy,
> My little babby,
> Dance to your daddy,
> My little lamb.

Once children are enjoying the fact that they can both hear, see and make up their own alliteration and rhymes it will be a pleasure to look at and talk about the many regular letter strings or combinations that occur in various positions in words. Sometimes these strings will be familiar end rhymes like 'sing' and 'king', or digraphs like 'ch', 'th' and 'sh', or the double vowel patterns 'ee', 'ea', 'ou', 'oo' and so on.

There is a very worrying aspect to this discussion of close encounters with words! In practice it can degenerate into the most pointless and unenjoyable 'phonics' work which is neither accurate in its insights about phonology (see Chapter 1) nor focused on stimulating children's love of language and books. Most of my examples have come from nursery rhymes and other traditional sources and this is because early encounters with words should be pleasurable, playful and permeating the child's day (please note the alliteration!). Literacy is *not* to be confined to set times and lessons but is a 24-hour commitment. Too formal an approach to literacy in the early years is a recipe for disaster.

Later stages of early literacy

There are several aspects of literacy which have not been discussed in this chapter and this is because they are later developments. Among these are such matters as reading and understanding non-fiction; writing and redrafting; 'authoring' or creating stories and books; critical appreciation of literature; and handwriting. Chapter 5 is devoted to case studies of work in two early years settings and will tackle some of these later stages in literacy development as they occur in the particular settings.

The role of the adult in supporting early literacy

The role of adults as literacy partners is crucial as young children become aware of literacy in their communities and of the part it plays in the lives of their carers and families. Young children will need adults who act as *literacy informants*, telling them what print 'says', and as *literacy demonstrators* who show them how to write themselves. They also need adults as scribes who will write for them and at their dictation, adults as *reading partners* who share books with them, and adults who are *literacy role models* who value literacy and use it in their own lives. Finally, it is clear that young children need adults to be *literacy facilitators* who provide the time, opportunities and materials for literacy to happen and for children and print of all kinds to get together.

This may appear to be a fairly daunting list of roles for adults, but we do not all have to be good at all of these things. We do have to be *aware* of them, and very active in cooperating to ensure that a variety of adult carers, professionals and educators together meet the children's literacy needs.

Provision and activities

- *Materials and tools*   As indicated in the previous chapters, babies and children need books (see the starter list at the end of Chapter 3). In homes and small group settings children need easy access to collections of paper, including 'waste' paper of all kinds (computer printouts, wallpaper scraps, old diaries); card, chalkboards, offcuts of hardboard, clean paper bags, used envelopes, unused forms and applications etc. Larger group settings and schools will also be able to use these materials and supplement them with paper of various kinds and some blank books, although school exercise books and lined paper will impose unhelpful restrictions on young children's mark making, experimental writing and investigations of print. Markers of many kinds should be provided, including brushes and paint, plain and coloured pencils, felt pens, biros, wax crayons, chalks and charcoal. Thick pencils and chubby crayons are not the only markers young children need – they also wish to write like grown-ups and enjoy handling fine markers and delicate colours.
- *Places*   The organization of literacy materials and tools and the provision of comfortable places in which to write and read are important literacy matters. In home settings it is possible for children and carers to find their own favourite spots for reading and for small collections of books to be kept in a special corner, a box or on a shelf. Similarly, it is only necessary to keep a good collection of paper, other materials and markers in cartons, carrier bags or drawers and cupboards accessible for the children. Larger group settings must give more thought to planning literacy areas and the storage of materials for many children. Most professional carers and educators attempt to create 'literacy workshops' in their settings where the children will find plenty of books in cosy,

attractive reading corners and areas; some tables and desks for writing at; perhaps a computer and software; ample collections of print from the outside world (magazines and newspapers, letters, maps, shopping lists, recipes, carrier bags, programmes, forms, cartons and labels, greetings cards etc.); all the tools, markers and paper they need stored in carefully labelled boxes, on shelves or in baskets and other storage units. Other important materials which can support and develop early literacy are audio and video tapes of stories and favourite books, as well as 'story props' (discussed below).

- *Things to do*   Many suggestions for early literacy work with young children have been made in the course of this chapter and it should be absolutely clear that the highest priority must be given to sharing books with children, telling and reading stories to them and providing continual opportunities for drawing, painting, mark making and writing. To these basics four other early literacy activities can be added: making books; making story props; shared reading; and shared writing.

Making books often happens fairly spontaneously when a child folds a sheet of paper in half and calls it 'a book'. Adults can encourage this by folding and stapling or sewing sheets of paper together. Children can draw pictures for their first books, write in them and stick in pictures, postcards and photos. It is well worth taking photos for these books and in group settings we can make bigger books for small groups of children to record shared experiences (e.g. 'Our visit to the street market'). Families and individual carers can make books with their children which are of great personal and cultural relevance, although they may be shared with other children. Many people like to start book making with a simple zig-zag of concertina-folded strong paper or card. A few photographs of relatives, holidays or previous homes can be put in a scrapbook with simple written captions, such as 'Granpa lives in Shanghai' or 'Mummy lived in this house in Delhi when she was a little girl'. Or, a book can be made about the birth of a new brother or sister or the celebration of a wedding or any other culturally significant life event. It is important that a family's own written language, apart from English, is used in these personal books. English translations can be added later if appropriate or necessary. Book making teaches children that they can be authors and raises the self-esteem of children and families (they have joined the literacy club). It also teaches the specialized language and conventions of literacy: pictures, print, pages, cover, title, author, illustrator and words.

Making story props is a way of bringing stories in books alive in a very special way for young children and also of providing them with 'props' to support their own recall and retelling of the stories. A prop can be an audio tape version of a book (particularly effective if the recording is made by a parent, carer or teacher); it can be some drawings of the characters in the book, backed with velcro or magnetic tape for moving about on a metal surface or a felt-covered board. Props can also be soft toys or puppets (a Spot, a teddy, a rag doll); and props can be objects which play a part in the book (e.g. hot water bottle, shopping basket, three spoons and three bowls).

Shared reading enables us to share a book with a group of young children so that they share their varying degrees of knowledge about narratives, books, print, words and sounds with each other. This pooling of reading knowledge is further enriched by the adult reader who adds her or his skills to the discussions and guides the children's responses by drawing their attention to details in pictures and print – for example, conventions of page layout (Where do I go next? What do I have to read?), punctuation (What is that mark for?) and recurring patterns like alliteration and rhyme. This sharing also helps children to make predictions about plot, motives and word meanings. Shared reading is now an established practice in educational settings and very large versions of many favourite children's picture books are easily available in high street bookshops. These are known as 'big books' and their size is designed to ensure that every child in a group can see the finest details of print and illustrations. Shared reading is every bit as valuable when carried out at home between children and parents or other family members.

Shared writing is more commonly practised in educational group settings and it adds to children's knowledge of the conventions of writing as they begin to move from early mark making to experiments with signs, letters and spellings. The adult writes (acts as scribe) on a flip chart, small chalkboard or on large sheets of paper attached to a small easel and uses a bold marker pen. The group discusses what they wish to write about, and this should arise from their shared interests and experiences. The adult scribe is the children's literacy adviser and helps them to form their individual spoken contributions into linked phrases and sentences which can be recorded in writing. This teaches the children a great deal about the differences between speech and writing. As the scribe writes he or she shares every aspect of her or his thinking and planning out loud with the children/authors (Where do I start? Do I use a capital letter? How do I spell that? What does it start with? Do I put a full stop now?). The children can see how a text grows, what decisions writers have to make, why conventions of punctuation and spelling are so important and why it is essential to rewrite things to make our meanings absolutely clear.

Further reading

Browne, A. (1996) *Developing Language and Literacy 3–8*. London: Paul Chapman.

Campbell, R. (1996) *Literacy in Nursery Education*. Stoke-on-Trent: Trentham Books.

Hall, N. and Robinson, A. (1995) *Exploring Writing and Play in the Early Years*. London: David Fulton.

Kress, G. (1996) *Before Writing: Rethinking the Paths to Literacy*. London: Routledge.

Miller, L. (1996) *Towards Reading*. Buckingham: Open University Press.

Language, literature and literacy in two early years settings

These schools are communities, mutual communities of learners/
doers/imaginers, all engaged in exploring the world of the possible,
constructing new experiences. Not only children and teachers, but also
families, and even interested visitors like me . . . Everybody is lending
a hand, doing a job, trying to make sense. It is a community of mutual
interest – a model of what a community based on respect should be,
where everything develops through interactive processes of
continuous negotiation between different perspectives and points of
view . . . This is what I found in the infant-toddler centers and
preschools of Reggio Emilia.

(Bruner 1996: 117)

The achievements and commitment of the children and the communities
that support the Reggio Emilia early years schools in Italy cannot be too
highly praised and they are a source of inspiration to practitioners and
families around the world. The two case studies which make up this
chapter are a reminder that we do not necessarily have to travel to Italy in
order to find early years settings that are communities of respect where
children, teachers, families, helpers and visitors are learners, doers and
imaginers. But we may have to keep an open mind about the possibility
that these case studies represent an endangered species of early years
practice in the UK.

The settings chosen are rather different in that one is a particular state-maintained nursery school in north London while the other case study is based on the work of two or three schools in the private sector that are part of an international philosophical and educational movement: the Rudolf Steiner Waldorf Schools (usually referred to as Steiner Waldorf Education). This difference might cause problems in a traditional approach to so-called objective 'research', but these are case studies of early years education 'in action'. They are examples of actual practice and attempt to capture the essence of what goes on, 'catching the moments' as it were – somewhat like the child observations scattered through the previous chapters. Of course it is not simply a matter of describing the 'happenings', it is equally important to try and gain some insights into what the 'doers' themselves – children and adults – think about what they are doing, feeling, making and experiencing. But let us go and visit the settings . . .

Hampden Way Nursery School

Some background notes

Hampden Way Nursery School is situated in a residential area of north London where the residents are mostly home owners, although a small percentage of the children attending the school live in local authority rented accommodation. The building was put up during the Second World War as a temporary day nursery for the young children of munitions workers.

There are two classrooms of unequal size connected by a bathroom area; a staff room; a small kitchen; two offices and a sloping garden with grassed and tarmac areas, reached from the rear of the building by stone steps and a slope. The two areas immediately outside each classroom are roofed over to provide a sheltered play space in wet weather. The main problem which this old and 'temporary' building presents is a serious lack of space and there is a consequent need to double up on the functions and use of the staff room and the offices.

The outside garden area is viewed as an integral and complementary part of the learning environment and is currently a focus for development. The permanent facilities include a large sandpit, a digging pit for children's gardening, a small pond, an old swing frame, a pergola, a large wooden train and a large house-like structure incorporating a slide.

There are 100 children on role, 50 attending the morning sessions and 50 attending the afternoon sessions, including 7 children who attend full-time. The children and their families encompass the rich social and cultural diversity found in all large cities, but the largest ethnic minority groups are Greek and Greek Cypriot (18 per cent). Most of these children are third generation British and speak fluent English and Greek. Some children of Chinese and Asian origin enter the school with little or no English (6–10 per cent) but on leaving are usually competent in understanding and speaking English. Children are admitted twice yearly and their ages on entry range from 3 years and 1 month to 3 years and 8 months, and many leave well before their fifth birthday to enter local primary schools.

The school staff consists of three teachers (including the head and her deputy), three nursery nurses and two part-time welfare assistants working with children with designated special educational needs, a part-time school secretary, a mealtime supervisor and a cleaner.

The practitioners in this school would probably describe themselves as working in the well-established traditions of British nursery education, with its strong emphasis on knowledge of child development and the provision of a developmentally appropriate curriculum in the early years. This includes viewing the *processes* of learning as of great significance, rather than focusing exclusively on narrow outcomes or results. It is an approach often described as 'child-centred', although many practitioners prefer to call it learner-centred or even 'child-sensitive' (Bredekamp and Rosegrant 1992).

This commitment to developmentally appropriate practice (Bredekamp 1987) at Hampden Way is reflected in the organization of teaching, material resources and the school environment. The latter is organized around curriculum resource areas spanning both classrooms, although a book area is included in both rooms. The children have access to a language and literacy area, a listening area, an arts workshop, science and mathematics areas, sand and water play provision, large block play and small construction areas, a music area, a home corner, small-world play, malleable materials and all the resources of the garden. Children are encouraged to use the resources throughout the school, take care of them and use them appropriately. The staff aim to foster the children's independence and encourage them to make connections in their learning, recognizing that 'learning is not compartmentalized' in the early years.

The whole staff team works on a rota basis covering both rooms and the garden, and while the teachers lead the teams the nursery nurses participate fully in all aspects of the school's organization and practice.

The broad approach to language and literacy

Over the past two years the school staff have focused on the children's language and literacy development, analysing their current practices and drawing up plans to ensure that this fundamental area is fostered most effectively. The following written comments by the headteacher set out the school's broad approach to language and literacy:

> A wealth of observations of children talking, representing and playing have informed our practice, together with research evidence and case studies of young children that draw on evidence from a wide variety of cultural and social backgrounds (Torrey 1973; Heath 1983; Bissex 1984; Payton 1984). All this research and knowledge convinced us that children are active in constructing their own theories about language. They ask questions of themselves, as well as of adults, using situational [everyday] print as a resource. Although not directly instructed, children are supported by adults who talk with them, responding to their questions and offering further information.
>
> Vygotsky (1978) refers to the 'zone of proximal development' which looks at a child's current stage of development and at the level of her [sic] potential development that can be achieved with appropriate guidance and support from adults. We believe that it is a question of 'tuning in' to children and enabling them to take the next step forward in their learning. Bruner (1983) called this 'scaffolding' children's learning.
>
> The guiding principles for the school's practice that emerged from our discussions of research and practice were that children should:
>
> - be active participants in their own learning;
> - have their own learning strategies and experience valued, supported and extended;
> - have many opportunities to interact with sensitive and supportive adults;
> - have many opportunities for play and talk;
> - be in an environment that reflects their social and cultural identities;
> - be in an environment that is rich in a wide variety of print;
> - develop their language and literacy in a meaningful and integrated way.

Many conflicting theories about the ways in which children learn are now current. The effect of the 'desirable learning outcomes' has often been to narrow down the early years curriculum and to make judgements about children's learning in terms of the final product, or the outcome. For example, too early an emphasis is often being placed on the formation of neat regularly-formed letters. Yet it is the process of learning that is of fundamental importance. Bissex refers to the 'child's inner teacher' (1984). Children's learning needs to be skilfully supported and extended, or 'scaffolded', so that their own very effective structures which enable them to experiment, predict, test, amend and construct rules can flourish. In other words, we must have faith in the child.

Talking and listening

The school strives to create a setting in which children can talk freely with each other and with adults in spontaneous conversations and through role play. The provision of such things as play telephones and an outdoor telephone kiosk provide opportunities for talking and listening in a variety of real-life situations. The two boys in the kiosk shown in figure 5.1 are talking to each other and a third is eavesdropping on the conversation – an important real-world listening skill! In this nursery setting opportunities for private one-to-one conversations between adult and child are seen as

Figure 5.1   At the telephone kiosk.

vitally important and professional educators, students, visitors and parents can be found talking to newly enrolled children, explaining the use of the computer and discussing the route to the school with the aid of a local street map. The children are given time to talk, to think aloud and find and experiment with words.

This careful planning for collaborative talk and listening between children and between adults and children reflects the professional staff's understanding that talk is of fundamental importance in all areas of children's learning as well as being the foundation of literacy. Guidance on a wide range of provision and activities for talking and listening and on what adults can do to support it is displayed around the school and has been incorporated into an album of photos and guidelines created especially for parents by a nursery nurse (see Appendix II).

Stories, storytelling and books

The children are given many opportunities to experience the joy of stories. Stories are read and told at group story times at the end of sessions and are also told and read on request to individuals or small groups during the course of the day. Story sessions include poetry, rhyme and songs as the children love to play with words, hear them rhyming in poems and nonsense rhymes and create their own verses, jingles and tongue-twisters. The children are given many opportunities to look at books independently so that they can view themselves as readers, or take on the role of storytellers with their friends, or just retreat from the demands of group life. In Figure 5.2 we see a 3-year-old who has just started at the school. She already has a deep love of books and the little bookcase in the hallway provides an oasis, away from the activity of the classrooms, where children can study books quietly.

Books are everywhere in the school and children can be found reading to each other round every corner, often interrupting their play to browse through a favourite book or create a fantastic tale from the pictures. In this literary early years setting it is not unusual to see a child dressed in all the glory of an old bridesmaid's dress put down her doll baby and big handbag, put her feet up on a stool and have a quiet 'read'. Similarly, two 4-year-old 'space travellers' paused in their explorations of the universe to read books to each other, while still keeping their helmets on – ready for the next 'lift off'.

In a setting so permeated by stories, role play, books and the love of literature it is not surprising to find the stories the children know constantly re-created by them, with the aid of story props which enable them to understand, recall and re-enact texts. Most props are made by the staff, but a few

Figure 5.2   A 3-year-old reading in the book corner in the hallway.

are purchased and some are improvised by the children. The story props for *The Three Billy Goats Gruff* (see Figure 5.3) were set up in the block area by the staff because the story was such a favourite with the children. The children enacted the story, moving the models and varying the pitch of their own voices to indicate characters, while a student nursery nurse turned the pages of the big book. The furry lion, owned by the boy in the two-tone sweatshirt, became the troll in preference to the one originally set up by the staff.

The children regularly hear stories and rhymes in languages other than English. This is because parents are asked to come in and share their languages and literary culture with the children. Clearly this is an aspect of working in partnership with families and the community (see Chapter 7), but it also indicates that the school values ethnic, cultural and linguistic diversity. These kinds of experiences enrich the language curriculum and demonstrate the school's respect for what families and children bring to the educational process.

Figure 5.3 Playing with the story props for *The Three Billy Goats Gruff*.

Books are available throughout the school, including the hallway, the headteacher's room and imaginative play areas like the 'home corner'. Here there are books, magazines, comics and written materials that the children might find in their own homes. The staff choose books that will reflect aspects of the children's own backgrounds and experiences, as well as the traditional tales of many cultures and the wilder fantasies of many modern picture books. They also look for repetitive texts and pop-up devices which encourage attention, prediction, memorization and an awareness of the permanent features of written texts. Before reading a book the staff make a point of referring to the book's author and illustrator so that the children can appreciate that real people write and illustrate books. The children are encouraged to make their own books – either individually or in groups – and the themes often arise from a favourite story book or a special experience. Some children dictate their own story to a member of staff who writes it down, some make marks or draw pictures for their books, and some use their own developmental writing strategies to create text. It is not surprising that at Hampden Way stories spill over into all aspects of the curriculum, as when a group of children exploring the local park set off through the 'swishy swashy' long grass announcing that they were 'going on a bear hunt'. Or when three children playing on the horizontal ladder of the climbing frame became the Three Billy Goats Gruff 'trip trapping' over the bridge.

Play

The fact that stories and books become fully integrated into the children's imaginative play has already been indicated, and the school's provision of everyday written materials in the home corner, as well as play 'office' areas with telephones, notepads, stationery and directories confirms an approach to literacy which is thoughtful and play-based. The power and fascination of literacy is demonstrated in many examples of the children's play:

- a 'Book a Ride' board in the garden on which children write their names to record that they are waiting to ride one of the tricycles;
- plastic magnetic letters arranged on the classroom floor by one child to create the names of his entire family including Rob the dog;
- painting and drawing materials, often used to incorporate letters and numerals in patterns, scribbles and representational pictures;
- spontaneous use of a sharp tool to make letter-like marks on flattened clay, as well as the formation of the letters of a child's name from rolled 'worms' of clay;
- buckets of water and decorating brushes put in the garden for children who 'painted' the outside apparatus 'in role' as decorators – James drew himself on the dry tarmac; a splendidly life-size tadpole-like figure!

The use of large blocks and bricks also has its literacy dimension as writing materials are always available nearby and the children often draw and write about their constructions. Interpreting and using symbols of many kinds is a fundamental aspect of literacy development. A child of 4 years and 6 months made a flag and insisted that it should be hoisted on a post in the playground. With the assistance of a student nursery nurse he devised a pulley system using rope and card toilet roll centres, and finally drew a plan of his construction.

Emergent writing and reading

The gradual emergence of young children's literacy understandings and skills out of real needs to read and write and meaningful experiences of literacy in action are amply demonstrated by all these examples. The staff of this nursery school do not leave the emergence of literacy to chance but plan for it and nurture it. The children are given the tools that adults use (biro, word processor, clock, angle poise lamp) and the staff themselves are 'models' of literate people because they take care to read and write in front of the children (doing office work with the door open; looking at a book while the children settle down for a story session). The nursery environment is rich in print: there are calendars, food boxes and news-papers in the home corner; school signs and information are written in the several home languages of the children; labels on the equipment are made by the children as well as the staff; and the children have their own name labels to use purposefully. For example, they 'register' for each session by placing their names on a special board as they arrive and the names stay there as useful and significant resources and references all through the session.

Just as literacy serves real purposes for the adults and children in this nursery, so the children themselves are treated as readers and writers from the beginning. They are not in any 'pre-' stage and their initial mark making is treated as part of a learning continuum that, if 'scaffolded' appropriately, will lead to conventional writing and reading with under-standing. All the stages of the children's mark making and writing are dis-played in the school to show the children that their work is valued and to help their parents understand the developmental processes of literacy. Even the displayed alphabet frieze which can be a helpful reference point for young readers and writers is particularly meaningful because it has been made up from the children's photographs and first names:

Dd   Dimitri   Damon   Daniel   Dario   Diane

Reading and writing for real purposes – some snapshots

A group of children had been observing frogs in the small pond and this included a spontaneous recording of the experience as observational drawings 'from life' on the tarmac. The protective guard was replaced over the pond but Robert (3 years 10 months) felt that it was important to make a notice saying 'Danger, deep water' and place it over the mesh. He chose black paper himself and used chalk, on the suggestion of an adult, so that his message could be seen (see Figure 5.4).

Mawluda (4 years 1 month) drew some interesting 'boxes' after watch-ing the teacher mark the register (see Figure 5.5). Mawluda is from Afghanistan, her first language is Farsi and, as yet, she speaks very little English. On the day that she apparently represented the distinctive format of the school register she also created the written communication shown in Figure 5.6. The written forms of Farsi may well be influencing her early writing as the other examples of her daily spontaneous writing, including tiny drawings, indicate (see Figure 5.7). It is clear that Mawluda uses writ-ten forms to make sense of the puzzling new world of school, to explore the potential of written communications and to engage in an important high-status activity.

Figure 5.4 Robert's warning notice.

Figure 5.5 Mawluda's 'register'.

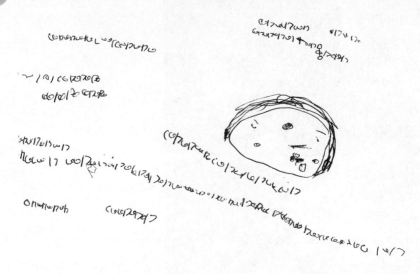

Figure 5.6   Mawluda's 'writing'.

Figure 5.7   Mawluda's 'tiny drawings'.

Makoto is the 3-year-old child seen reading alone in Figure 5.2. She is a Japanese speaker who daily creates detailed drawings of her family: mother, father, younger sister and herself (see Figure 5.8). The two circles on the top of the children's hair depict the bows that the two sisters wear each day. This daily drawing activity is for the young child a powerful way of representing, remembering and recording 'who I am', 'who I belong to' and 'what I do'.

Figure 5.8   3-year-old Makoto's family.

A television listings magazine was placed in the home corner and Sarah (3 years 5 months) became very involved with this, studying pictures of familiar television characters, looking at the text and saying when the programmes were on.

A music manuscript board was put up in the music resource centre and the children soon became adept at writing lines and bold 'blobs' reminiscent of crotchets and quavers.

A parent donated a computer to the school and the simple word-processing system offers the children another means of creating and reading texts. It also offers a line of communication to children with impaired communication skills, particularly those who show great reluctance to use paper and pencil.

Records and assessment[1]

The staff plan carefully for the development of the children's language and literacy and this planning is shaped by detailed records of the children's progress and interests. Profiles of individual children are built up using information gained through:

- ongoing discussions with parents (initiated on a home visit);
- child observations (both planned and targeted at individuals, and spontaneous);
- collected samples of children's work (drawings, paintings, writing, photographs).

Individual reviews of progress take place termly and are shared with parents. Final profiles, written in the child's last term, are also shared with parents and forwarded to the appropriate primary school.

Children are observed regularly throughout their period in the school. An observation register is kept by the teacher to ensure that all the children are observed. Staff meet together weekly to discuss 'targeted' children.

Newly admitted children are 'targeted' for observation after approximately six weeks to provide an early assessment of their present stage of learning and ongoing development. Areas of concern can be identified and development more closely monitored. Copies of planning and child development review sheets are shown in Appendix II. Caution is adopted in all of these early assessment procedures in order to minimize hasty and inappropriate judgements.

Steiner Waldorf Education

Some background notes[2]

Steiner Waldorf is an international educational movement with some 730 schools, over 1500 kindergartens and 60 teacher training institutes in 56 countries. The general philosophy reflects a central European tradition of valuing childhood for its own sake, but the movement's direct inspiration is found in the writings of the Austrian philosopher Rudolf Steiner (1861–1925). The emphasis of the approach is developmental with three distinctive stages of childhood recognized and supported by an appropriate curriculum: early years (0–7), childhood (7–14) and adolescence and early adulthood (14–21). These stages connect with a threefold 'hand, heart and head' concept of education which relates to the development of the corresponding faculties of willing, feeling and thinking in the individual. In the first phase the emphasis is on the *will*. The child first encounters the world through her or his own willed bodily activity and gradually acquires a repertoire of increasingly refined skills as movement and coordination are brought under control. In the second phase the affective or *feeling* realm predominates and the third phase culminates in the development of mature adult *thinking*.

The early years phase is seen as a period of active learning in which children play and imitate, absorb and reflect on their experiences in a secure, caring and structured environment. Teaching is always by example rather than instruction at this stage. There is a clear moral and spiritual – although undenominational – emphasis and a strong belief in social responsibility, routine and community. The curriculum is planned so as to be sensitive to the developmental needs of the individual child and play is valued as a significant mode of learning during this period when children 'think' with their entire being. The need to grasp things physically (with the will) is a precursor to the later grasping of concepts (with the thinking). Only when new capabilities for abstract thinking appear at around the seventh year are children considered to be physically, emotionally and intellectually ready for formal instruction.

The aims and objectives outlined in the Steiner Waldorf early years curriculum statement are:

- to recognize and support each stage of child development;
- to provide opportunities for children to be active in meaningful imitation;
- to work with rhythm and repetition;
- to encourage personal, social and moral development;
- to provide an integral learning experience;
- to encourage learning through creative play and to support physical development;
- to encourage children to know and love the world;
- to provide a safe, child-friendly environment;
- to work with parents.

Most of these aims are familiar enough to parents and early years workers but two are less so and need expanding. The notion of 'meaningful imitation' relates to the Steiner view that young children learn by example, by imitating and modelling their behaviour on what goes on around them. Thus a Steiner kindergarten is a community of 'doers', whether it be baking their own bread or cleaning a room, and it follows that adult carers and workers must always strive to be worthy of imitation (both morally and practically). This is not a naive theory of mindless copying but an awareness of the complex ways in which the young need to be involved and initiated into the ways of their communities.

Working with 'rhythm and repetition' indicates the central role played by rhythm in Steiner Waldorf educational principles. At one level this is reflected in the high priority given to music and poetic language in Steiner schools, but it goes deeper. Children are seen to need the reassurance of continuity and regularity, so great stress is put on such orderly rituals as activity and rest times, tidying up and 'circle times' (for stories), seasonal celebrations and birthdays. These rhythmic patterns help children to live with change, find their place in the world and begin to understand the past, present and future. Repetition is seen to strengthen memory and establish continuity and, in the case of stories and rhymes, gives the children many opportunities to become familiar with new material and reflect on its meanings.

In the UK there are 56 Steiner Waldorf kindergartens and 27 schools, and all are privately funded. Most of the material in the following case study came from the Rosebridge Steiner Kindergarten in Cambridge. The school occupies the ground floor of a converted house and has a garden with a paved area, a sandpit, a gardening area and space for play and large constructions. This area is equipped with planks, steps, branches and logs which the children use to build see-saws, slides, ever-changing obstacle courses and even a merry-go-round. Figure 5.9 shows children building and improvising with similar materials in the Christchurch Gardens Kindergarten in Reading.

Figure 5.9 'Building' in the garden.

At Rosebridge there are plans to create, in partnership with parents, an organic garden which will produce vegetables to sell for kindergarten funds. The school has two teachers and places for 14 children, plus a current waiting list of 43 for September 1998. There is evidence of lots of domestic and imaginative play, cooking and baking, provision for music, drawing and painting, wax and clay modelling and 'endless construction' (a teacher's words) using large blocks and kindergarten furniture, miniature worlds (farms, towns, trains) and the garden equipment. Rhythm and ritual are established by having a weekly pattern of activities: Monday is baking day, Tuesday is painting, Wednesday is crafts, Thursday is cooking and Friday is cleaning and polishing. The seasons of the year are celebrated and this includes the great festivals of Easter, May Day, Harvest, Michaelmas, Diwali and Christmas. A very great occasion is made of every child's birthday, with a crown to wear and candles, flowers, cake, birthday verses and the participation of the parents.

The broad approach to language and literacy

The Steiner Waldorf early years curriculum is a totally integrated one and any attempt to separate out the elements of language and literacy distorts the full picture. Therefore the following comments from an experienced practitioner and adviser (Jenkinson 1997a) focus on the philosophy and principles which shape developmentally appropriate education in Steiner Waldorf kindergartens.

Contemporary life puts children under increasing pressure to grow up as quickly as possible and current research shows that children in coercive early learning programmes suffer from high levels of anxiety, stress, sleep problems and low self-esteem. Forcing children to learn skills before they are maturationally ready is both ineffective and counterproductive. Full perceptual processing ability is not complete in a child of four years old and we respect the process of gradual development which allows the aural and visual senses to mature slowly over time ... We feel that accelerated formal learning is achieved at a cost – and our concern is that 'hot house' children may prove to be less robust in the long term. We believe that each stage of child development has unique qualities to impart to the child and should be experienced fully before the next stage is embarked upon.

... we concentrate on pre-literacy and pre-numeracy skills, skills which are 'caught rather than taught' ... our children have good phonological awareness, their oral skills are strong, their vocabulary is extensive and by their seventh year they are ready and physiologically *able* to learn. By creating a friendly environment, where each child feels safe and not under pressure to perform, the kindergarten teacher weaves a tapestry of learning experiences for the child – all the elements of which have context and meaning and arise from the life of the kindergarten itself. Through familiar events, which make sense to the children, at *their* level – and which relate to the well-ordered kindergarten daily, weekly and yearly rhythms – children cook, bake, garden, paint, draw; they listen quietly to stories told to them by their teachers, they celebrate festivals together and they learn to consider the needs of others. They learn for life from life. All learning is practical and substantive. Our children do involve themselves in activities such as making their own books; many write their names and a few discover reading, but most are busy with their own 'serious work' and we support their self-initiated activity. To quote Rousseau, 'What is the use of inscribing on their brains a list of symbols which mean nothing to them? They will learn the symbols when they learn the things signified' (Rousseau [1762] 1991: 76).

Talking and listening

Steiner kindergartens take a particular approach to talking and listening in the early years curriculum. The emphasis is on listening to and developing an appreciation for live music (lyre, flute, human voice); listening to traditional stories and stories created from daily experiences; learning songs and singing games with mimed and verbal responses; creating role play scenarios and drama; recalling experiences and developing narrative and conversational skills; performing puppet shows; and reciting nursery rhymes to develop the rhythms of language and a feeling for sound and melody.

The musical and poetic qualities of language are emphasized by the use of verses and rhymes to mark the daily, seasonal and celebratory routines of kindergarten life. Thus a retelling of a traditional fairy tale may be preceded by a familar song which sets the mood and encourages listening:

Mother of the fairy tale take me by your silver hand,
Sail me in your silver boat, sail me silently afloat.
Mother of the fairy tale take me to your shining land.

And a very popular blessing is usually sung before meals:

Blessings on the blossom, blessings on the fruit,
Blessings on the leaf and stem, blessings on the root.

After this blessing adults and children all join hands around the table and say together 'Blessings on the meal'.

Undoubtedly the use of language in Steiner schools is marked by attention to gesture, well-formulated speech and musicality, but there is also a remarkable liveliness and playfulness in the spontaneous conversations of children with each other and with adults. Some examples of play with language will be returned to in the comments on 'Play', but a few snippets of conversations will demonstrate the intellectual and social power of the oral curriculum in these kindergartens. Like young children everywhere they talk during meals, while they play, while they tidy up and while they cook. In this first example a group of children are baking Christmas bicuits at Wynstones Kindergarten in Gloucester.

Child 1:   We're making patterns on these biscuits.
Child 2:   We're having licks afterwards.
Joshua (5): We're not allowed to lick until we've done every single one.

A later conversation in the same school between Joshua (5) and a little girl (4) reveals both true logic (using if/then clauses) and a Hamlet-like awareness of folk myths and family loyalty:

Joshua: Ghosts are people who have just died.
Girl: My grandfather's just died.
Joshua: Then he must be a ghost.
                  Pause
Joshua: Ghosts are bad.
Girl: My grandfather wasn't bad.
Joshua: Then he won't be a ghost then, if you're bad you're a ghost.

As in all early years settings, the children frequently engage the adults in conversations which are creative and thought-provoking. The following exchange was recorded by Sally Jenkinson, Early Years Adviser, Steiner Education UK, in a personal communication:

A 4-year-old boy, Charles, asked me to come outside to see his 'bout'.

Sally: What do you mean Charles, what is a 'bout'?
Charles: It's a 'bout'.
Sally: Do you mean a belt to put round your waist?
Charles: No, I mean a 'bout'.

At this point Charles decided I just wasn't getting it, so he took me to the sandpit where a straight line and a circle had been carefully shaped out of the sand.

Charles: Look Sally [said with polite exasperation] it's a *round*-a bout.

Once I saw it, it all made sense. Relief and triumph were written all over Charles' face: I have made her understand – at last! It was as if a 'bout' were a place where things met and changed, a place where there might indeed be other kinds of bout: square bouts, or oblong bouts, for example. (We do have the expressions 'about turn' and 'thereabouts', so perhaps Charles was on to something.) He had a basic concept that a 'bout', as a noun, somehow stayed still whilst things happened in different ways around it, and he was intuitively following the rules of grammar which apply when adjectives describe nouns. Charles was searching for a way to name the (empty) space. This deeply thoughtful boy's father was an architect.

Stories, storytelling and books

The oral telling of stories and the development of children's narrative skills are major features of Steiner Waldorf education and although the formal teaching of reading is not begun until children are 6-plus, picture books with little or no text are used in some kindergartens. Sometimes a teacher will share a special book with a group of children and it is not unusual to find children looking at picture books and telling their own stories. Morning stories, however, are always 'told' rather than read to the children.

In another personal communication Sally Jenkinson writes:

An important feature of the kindergarten day is the story. The stories are drawn from a wide range of folk and fairy tales, as well as nature and seasonal stories (which follow the cycle of the year), stories about plants and animals, and stories of families and domestic life.

The telling of a story is always a special event in the kindergarten day. Traditionally the telling of folk tales marked the coming of night and created in the mind a different rhythm. Our stories are told to the whole kindergarten group and are sometimes acted out with gesture, song and movement in circle time. The beautifully chosen words, well-constructed narratives and deep underlying structures and patterns in the traditional tales are the child's first introduction to literature. We observe little customs such as lighting a candle, singing a special song or playing some lyre music, as a prelude to the story and to help the children leave the work of the day and enter the realm of the imagination.

The fairy stories are told because they paint beautiful pictures of our human feelings, as personified by the greedy wolf, the honest miller's son, the courageous youngest prince; they tell of trickery, treachery, cruelty and folly and give an overview of life. All the characters in one story make up a whole because all qualities, good and bad and everything in between, are an essential part of human nature . . . potential aspects of our own being.

Fairy tales also give the child access to a rich vocabulary of words and concepts. A 3-year-old child in the Wynstones Kindergarten, Gloucester, demonstrated her ability to make meaning out of her morning story by creating a new context to try out the words and phrases she had heard earlier. She took a little stand-up puppet doll and began to retell the story. As she carefully moved her puppet, who represented the good girl in the story, she was heard to say in a voice of great precision and emphasis and not without a dramatic flourish, 'She was a *paragon* of virtue . . .'. This small storyteller may not know the meanings of the individual words, but her understanding comes from the context in which she first heard the adult using them and now she uses them herself in her own speech, effortlessly demonstrating Bruner's 'scaffolding' and Vygotsky's 'zone of proximal development'.

It is not surprising to find the kind of fairy tale inspiration described above spilling over into all aspects of play in Steiner kindergartens and creating a complex web of the fantastic, the symbolic and the practical. In Figure 5.10 the two 4-year-old girls are princes dressed in capes and crowns, and they are feeding their horses. They had made their horses a sleeping corner with muslin representing hay and a large part of the game was taken up with discussions about what horses eat, how they sleep, how they should be cared for etc. The princes, Hester and Anna, wondered whether horses liked oats, hay or chestnuts. Having decided upon chestnuts they let the conkers in the basket remain as conkers (*horse*-chestnuts) and gave them to the horses as food.

Children in Steiner kindergartens are also very experienced in the crucial early literacy skill of creating a narrative, or story, about their own lives and families. This is supported by the practice of telling birthday stories. These are told on a child's birthday in the kindergarten (parents are invited and asked to supply all the crucial pre-kindergarten data), and incorporate personal biographical details into an ongoing story of the child's life. Sometimes an item from babyhood is brought in to illustrate the story and demonstrate how much the child has grown and developed in a few years. The story is brought up to date with the child's recent achievements in the kindergarten. The story is a warm celebration of the life of a child which can contribute to a sense of self-worth which lasts for years.

Figure 5.10   Princes feeding their horses.

Steiner Waldorf early years educators would argue that care and respect for books in their kindergartens are promoted by having only a few at a time in a special area of the room. Respect is encouraged by the adults' care of books and by such practices as wrapping a treasured book in its own special cloth to keep it safe. There is usually a parents' library in which books are available for loan and the children are familiar with this. Books are used extensively in the later stages of Steiner education.

Play

'In our Steiner Waldorf Kindergartens, we are conscious of the very real threat to the world of the child and our concern is always to do the right thing at the right time – we recognise that children need time to play during their formative years' (Jenkinson 1997b: 48). This recognition is based on the widely accepted psychological theory that in play young children actually think by internalizing the processes of physical activities. Children's characteristic doing and thinking transform the most ordinary objects which come to hand into symbols which are rich in meanings: 'The ability to endow an object with a different order of existence is a genuine childhood talent' (Jenkinson 1997c: 105). A Steiner kindergarten will be full of playing children who improvise and talk about a range of narrative possibilities. For example:

- playing cafés and 'writing' menus;
- drawing maps and signposts for various games;
- writing 'letters' to each other on leaves in the garden;
- playing offices, with kindergarten chairs and tables positioned at different angles to create 'computers', 'cash registers', 'desks' etc.;
- using pine cones as 'telephones' and nuts, seeds and shells as 'money', and even making and signing paper credit cards.

Sometimes a play sequence develops into a large-scale event which gradually involves all the children in a cooperative fantasy. An example is shown in Figure 5.11. Caitlin (4 years 5 months), in the foreground, is making 'smoke' by carding wool and George (3 years 4 months) is steering the train by rotating a circular piece of wood. Other children had cut tickets from card and sold them in exchange for conker 'money'. There was a signalman with a stop-go board of correctly coloured circles (green and red) made by the children, and a guard's flag, also child-made. The children had gone on to make special tickets for going to Africa – yellow 'because it's hot', and to London – blue 'because it's cold'. This interesting sensitivity to appropriate colour symbolism in their representations went side-by-side with a very practical approach to planning journeys: a café was opened to serve drinks and fish and chips to passengers. Once the train was underway all the children made the loud and necessary 'choo-choo' noises and a real bell was rung as the train approached the station and when it was about to leave.

Play can also be very quiet and intense and only involve one or two players. Adam (4 years 6 months) and Katie (3 years 4 months) were witnessed preparing dinner in their pretend house, but this was part of an extended game which had begun with shops. Katie had been shopping and bought the fish and some chips (clothes pegs) and the two children made their own house and began preparing food. They talked about cooking methods: should the fish be fried, baked, roasted or barbecued? Barbecuing won and they made an elaborate cooking rack from a wooden circle across which they wound wool. The rack was placed over a 'fire' of red sheep's wool and conkers.

Figure 5.11   'The train'.

Play with language and a well-developed oral and phonological sensitivity can be found in many young children who attend Steiner Waldorf schools. Sally Jenkinson again:

> . . . 'the word' is created anew by every child. In the child's world, trees come 'timbering' down, caravans are 'car-wheel-housies', 'sheeps' live in fields and 'biscetti' is delicious with tomato sauce. (The same group called my assistant, who was tall, lanky but stately, 'Jean bean Elizabeth the Queen'!) In our kindergartens we hear children playing with language. They reverse words, they rhyme, they play with alliterative and onomatopoeic sounds and they create the most wonderful nonsense verse; they do this as naturally as they play with the shells and conkers around them.

Playfulness with language, and with people, comes through in the following observation:

> I sat next to a friendly boy who introduced himself to me by telling me that his name was 'M.O.T.' and that he was a car. I said that I thought he must be a very safe car. His friend, sitting nearby, turned to me with a withering look and said 'His name's Tom really ... that's M.O.T. backwards.' The two boys took great pleasure in their good-natured jest, especially as I had been so effectively caught out.
>
> (Jenkinson 1997a)

Emergent writing and reading

Although kindergarten teachers place no demands upon their children to produce letters or numbers, these often emerge spontaneously. The morning I visited the kindergarten was full of letter writing which the children were keen to show me, particularly when the window misted over, making an irresistible writing surface: 'This is my name, and this is mummy's name.' 'That's an A.' 'Those are my letters.' Numbers also scored well; fingers were spontaneously used to denote their owners' ages and children sang along with the teacher's counting rhymes. They took *great* pleasure in the alliteration and onomatopoeia of that morning's 'slithery slippery snake' rhyme.

(Jenkinson 1997a)

The above incidents in a Steiner Waldorf kindergarten could be repeated daily in any number of early years settings and private homes, but Steiner educators choose not to teach young children to 'recognize letters of the alphabet by shape and sound', or 'write their names with appropriate use of upper and lower case letters' (DfEE/QCA 1998). However, the children are familiar with the uses of writing in meaningful and important contexts such as their names on paintings, drawings, coat pegs and containers; the words of songs, verses and special books, or the many letters and notices for parents and teachers as well as other environmental print. On one occasion in the Sunlands Kindergarten, Stroud, two 4-year-olds had played together all morning and cooperated on a drawing of themselves. Esther (4 years 5 months) did most of it but Zoe (4 years 8 months) added her black hair, although she is a redhead, and black rain. Zoe then wrote the story on the back of the drawing: 'We went for a walk and it's raining and Tag [her dog] went in the pond'.

At this point in a child's literacy development the Steiner approach is distinctive.

It is at this stage that many educators begin to work directly with the child's emergent thinking and begin to teach literacy skills. The Steiner pre-school teacher, however, presses on with spoken language for longer, strengthening and enriching the foundations of the child's 'inner speech' (thought) so that the shift in the child's thinking which is necessary for the achievement of literacy (what psycholinguists call the shift to a 'metalinguistic consciousness') occurs from an enriched and strengthened position after approximately 7 years of age.

(Alwyn 1997: 23)

Emergent writing is supported in the Rosebridge Kindergarten in that if children ask for words the teachers will write them, but the greater emphasis is placed on lots of drawing and painting activities. They also do sewing, weaving, finger knitting, plaiting, modelling, candle making, gardening and woodwork. All these activities are considered good for developing eye–hand coordination, fine motor skills and later reading. The kindergarten, in common with all Steiner Waldorf schools, uses traditional German block wax crayons which give strong clear colours, can be easily grasped by small hands and can be used to create broad bands of colour or angled to produce curves and fine lines. After kindergarten, children in Class 1 of Steiner schools are taught literacy in a structured progression, beginning writing with the drawing of curves and straight lines and moving on to capital letters. Alphabetic letter forms are introduced by combining the shapes of consonants into representational drawings which provide phonological and visual clues, but also involve a story about each letter. For example, 'C' may be drawn as a cave and a narrative, perhaps about who lives in the cave and keeps a fire burning in it, will be integrated with tactile and rhythmic experiences of drawing 'C' in sand and in the air, or dancing its shape. At this stage the alphabet letters are represented as nouns and the vowels are usually shown as stars with their own gestures to accompany them. This literacy approach is always a progression from the whole to the parts and integrates sight, sound and movement.

Reading is prepared for in the kindergarten years by the establishment of all the oral and aural skills outlined above; by nurturing a love of literature and the patterned language of story, rhyme and poetry; by promoting and enriching children's narrative abilities; and by respecting and 'reading' children's pictures, gestures, movements and play so that an understanding of signs and symbols is developed. After kindergarten the children in Steiner Waldorf schools begin learning to read by using material they have themselves thought about, talked about and watched their teachers write, and only later move on to strategies for identifying unfamiliar material and using graded reading books.

In all their approaches to literacy, Steiner Waldorf educators are keenly aware of the long historical and cultural background to the human development of writing systems and do not rush children into using abstract symbols which are divorced from context and meaning. Their watchwords might fairly be summed up as 'better late than early' (Moore and Moore 1975). The unpressured context for literacy which is created allows children to explore systems of writing and other signs at their own pace – for example, a 'nearly' 4-year-old made some bold alphabet letters (see Figure 5.12).

At 5 years 6 months, Nicholas could explain his own complex work (see Figure 5.13) to the nursery assistant: 'This is a calendar. This one is today [points to one number "9"]. The drawing is a snowman and the person who made the snowman [drawn below the calendar]'. There are fascinating achievements in this example: Nicholas can write his name and he is

Figure 5.12   Bold alphabet letters by a 'nearly' 4-year-old.

Figure 5.13   Nicholas' calendar.

getting to grips with the conventions of calendars, the recording of time and the writing of numerals. Perhaps the snowman drawing is also a reflection of the many illustrated calendars which people now use in homes, offices, shops and schools.

Records and assessment

Steiner Waldorf kindergarten teachers keep records of children's development and evaluate their progress. This includes distinctively 'Steiner' assessments of physical development, music, drawing and cognition/thinking. The Rosebridge Kindergarten in Cambridge provides a leaving report that goes with the child when he or she moves on to state or private statutory schooling (there is no Steiner Waldorf school in the city), and this is accompanied by a statement on 'The Five Year Old Steiner Waldorf Child' (see Appendix III). The teachers meet weekly to discuss the progress of individual children and share their observations and insights. Individual case studies are documented and information is regularly shared with parents.

The essence of the case studies

The introduction to this chapter suggested that case studies can capture the essence of a human situation or institution, but these particular studies also offer alternative perspectives on early years practice. This is of considerable importance in a period of increasingly narrow definitions of childhood, learning, curriculum and literacy and the related regulations for early and statutory schooling. The following comments attempt to pin down what is shared by, and central to, the unique early years settings we have visited.

Both settings are strongly focused on child development and affirm that the first duty of early years educators is to tune-in to children, have faith in their powers as thinkers and social beings and by implication, understand what they are observing and know how to support and extend children's potential. This approach is backed up by recent research into the qualities and abilities of successful early years educators (Blenkin and Kelly 1997).

All the settings have a strong commitment to protecting and nurturing childhood and children's opportunities for play and symbolic representation of many kinds. This is based on a professional understanding that children's self-esteem and thinking is rooted in play and representation. It also reflects a crucial insight about literacy: that it is one of many symbolic systems for representing thinking and experience, so that puppets and stories, role play and block constructions, for example, can support the processes of writing and reading.

Both types of setting promote a rich oral (talking) and aural (listening) curriculum and a literary approach based on stories, rhyme and poetry. They do so because they know that the combination of spoken language, gossip and discussion, and patterned literary language provides a direct bridge to literacy. This oracy curriculum could be the basic 'basic' which makes all the difference in the early years.

Despite some distinctive differences around the issue of direct literacy instruction, both case studies are agreed on the need for early literacy to be encountered in meaningful contexts which relate directly to human purposes, interests and needs.

The role of the early years educator and carer is seen in essentially similar ways in these settings. Direct telling and instructing is less important or useful than engaging in shared learning alongside children so that joint meanings can be created. In this sense children's thinking and learning is 'scaffolded' and the adults are models of what it means to be talkers, thinkers, doers and imaginers.

The final and perhaps most urgent of all the themes to emerge from these case studies concerns the issue of imposing formal and so-called academic instruction on young children. There is growing contemporary evidence to add to the long-established view that early formal teaching damages young children's potential for creative thinking, undermines their self-esteem and social confidence, and may well turn them off from the later years of schooling. This issue is central to the discussion of the national frameworks for language which follows in Chapter 6.

Notes

1 Some of the planning and record-keeping formats used at Hampden Way are incorporated into the local authority planning document *The Barnet Early Years Record – A Framework for Planning*, published by the Inspection and Advisory Service for the London Borough of Barnet in June 1997, and some have been adapted from this document.

2 This section has drawn on material in *Steiner Waldorf Education: Aims, Methods and Curriculum*, edited by M. Rawson (1997), and has benefitted from the guidance of Sally Jenkinson, Early Years Adviser, Steiner Education, UK.

National requirements and frameworks for language and literacy

I arrived at the prison with 14 other inmates, all of whom had just been found guilty of breaking the rules of grammar. Ever since people started being a bit tougher with how they imposed education standards, more and more of us were put in the slammer.

(Iannucci 1998)

It is now the case that children as young as 3 and 4, as well as the 5s to 7s, are affected directly and indirectly by a combination of actual legislation and advisory frameworks which are shaping the teaching of language and literacy in early years settings and schools in England and Wales. Furthermore, as the earlier chapters of this book indicate, infants under the age of 3 years are directly affected by the views of language and literacy held by their carers, so that the current debates and legislation undoubtedly influence all of us – and our babies and toddlers – in ways we cannot easily predict. With this complex network of influences in mind the discussion in this chapter starts with an outline of the current legislation and advisory frameworks and then indicates some of the problems and challenges posed for the early years by these approaches. Next, a small-scale investigation of early years practitioners' views is presented and the chapter concludes with a reminder of some positive strategies to nurture young children's language and literacy development at home and in group settings.

National statutes, strategies and frameworks

Desirable outcomes for children's learning

Settings with 4-year-old children that applied to take the original nursery vouchers were required to meet the goals for learning set out in *Desirable Outcomes for Children's Learning* (SCAA 1996). In practice this meant that many independent early years providers, as well as maintained schools and nurseries, adopted these goals for children's learning on entry to compulsory education (legally, the term after the child's fifth birthday). Many 2- and 3-year-olds were also drawn into this 'curriculum' for the early years as providers felt obliged to teach the goals because they were, and still are, the criteria on which the inspections of early years settings are based. In a similar pattern of downward pressure for an earlier and earlier start to formal schooling many 4-year-olds in Reception classes have been drawn into the curriculum for Key Stage 1 of the National Curriculum.

The desirable learning outcomes remained after the abolition of nursery vouchers in 1997 and the revised edition of the requirements (DfEE/QCA, 1998) simply replaced all references to the voucher scheme with references to the new early years development partnership plans required from all local authorities. The unchanged outcomes cover children's development in six areas of learning: personal and social; language and literacy; mathematics; knowledge and understanding of the world; physical development; and creative development. There is an explicit emphasis on literacy, numeracy and personal and social development and a clear intention that these goals must 'dovetail' into Level 1 of the National Curriculum.

The language and literacy outcomes for 4-year-olds in England emphasize competence in English as soon as possible, developing competence in speaking and listening, and becoming readers and writers. These broad aims are then broken down into fine detail and include :

- listening attentively;
- using a growing vocabulary;
- listening and responding to stories, songs, nursery rhymes and poetry;
- making up stories and taking part in role play;
- enjoying books, handling them carefully and understanding how they are organized;
- knowing that words and pictures carry meaning;
- knowing that English is read from left to right and from top to bottom;
- associating sounds with patterns in rhymes, and with syllables, words and letters;
- recognizing own names and some familiar words;

- recognizing letters of the alphabet by shapes and sounds;
- in writing, using pictures, symbols, familiar words and letters to communicate meaning, and showing awareness of some of the different purposes of writing;
- writing own names with appropriate use of upper and lower case letters.

This list of goals is a mixture of good sense and excessive and insensitive detail, wrapped up in a culturally and linguistically narrow package. Many children write and read with their families from right to left and their names have written forms in which upper and lower case letters are inappropriate. Many enthusiastic early readers sit on piles of books and chew the corners off their favourite volumes! Meanwhile, in officially bilingual Wales, desirable outcomes are introduced with a poem in Welsh celebrating the imaginative powers of young children, and a paragraph on the importance of play (Curriculum and Assessment Authority for Wales 1996). Moreover, the six goals are also different in their details: language, literacy *and Communication Skills* are described as crucial to the child's intellectual, emotional and social learning and a wide range of significant experiences are listed, including:

- enjoying marking and basic writing;
- using marking implements for painting, drawing, writing and scribbling;
- discussing individual and group *play* and intentions;
- identifying and explaining events illustrated in pictures;
- understanding that written symbols have sound and meaning.

Since 1996 the official approach to assessing desirable outcomes during early years inspections in England has hardened and at the end of the first year there were calls for more systematic treatment of phonic work, letter recognition, name writing and reading familiar words (Ofsted 1997). This linked with a general tightening of the approach to literacy, is discussed below.

National Curriculum Key Stage 1

In theory, Key Stage 1 of the National Curriculum (DfE 1995) applies to children who have completed the Reception year and are aged 6 and 7. However, different summer and winter birth months, the problems of large class numbers or very small numbers of children in rural schools, the movements of families between countries and regions or in and out of private and voluntary care and education mean that many children get much less than a year of Reception. Whatever the reasons, most Reception classes are definitely focused on working towards the Key Stage 1 attainment targets. The programmes of study for Key Stage 1 English (at the start of the National Curriculm we seemed to 'lose' language and literacy) cover the same topics as the later Key Stages, namely, speaking and listening and reading and writing. There is an emphasis in each topic, and at all key stages, on the study of language and on learning to speak and write standard English.

At Key Stage 1 speaking and listening require opportunities for children to tell stories, experience play and drama, read and listen to nursery rhymes and poetry, participate in discussions, describe events, and give reasons for opinions and actions. The 'key skills' are described as communicating effectively and listening to others with growing attention and concentration.

The orders for Key Stage 1 reading require extensive experiences of children's literature and the introduction of information texts, dictionaries and encyclopedias in print and on screen. The 'key skills' include the need for children to read with fluency, accuracy, understanding and enjoyment, but a major emphasis is put on the teaching of phonic knowledge, graphic knowledge (regular letter patterns), instant word recognition (sight vocabulary), grammatical knowledge about sentences and likely meanings, and contextual understanding based on the overall content of a book or other text.

Writing at Key Stage 1 emphasizes the value of a range of personal writing – from enjoyment and personal interest to remembering and communicating, and organizing and developing ideas. Children are to be given opportunities to write for a range of different purposes and different audiences (people or readers) and should be taught the characteristics of such different written forms as stories, diaries, lists, instructions, notices etc. The 'key skills' of writing are deemed to be confidence, independence, fluency, and accuracy in the area of composition. The remaining 'key skills' to be taught are of the secretarial kind: spelling, punctuation, and handwriting, all of which receive specific attention.

The National Curriculum also describes the required standards for children's 'performance' in terms of eight levels of increasing difficulty. At the end of Key Stage 1 most children are expected to 'perform' within the range of Levels 1 to 3, making an average achievement for a just-7-year-old around Level 2. There follows a summary of such an achievement, in the language of the National Curriculum for English document, but I have also added notes expressing some concerns and reservations because this document has *not* been planned primarily as a curriculum for language and literacy in the early years.

Speaking and listening: beginning to show confidence in talking and listening; speaking clearly and using a growing vocabulary; usually listens carefully and responds with increasing appropriateness to what others say; beginning to be aware that in some situations a more formal vocabulary and tone of voice are used.

But . . .

There are huge developmental differences between children in terms of confidence, clarity of diction and social use of what might be a considerable personal vocabulary. Young bilinguals may have two or more languages and be learning English as an additional spoken language. As a result, they may be reluctant to speak until they are confident. Cultural and social experiences will affect children's perceptions of 'formal' vocabulary and tone of voice (some hear it at home, some are frightened, alienated or confused by it). And why so much emphasis on listening and responding to others? Children become good communicators because they are respected and listened *to*.

Reading: reading of simple texts shows understanding and is generally accurate; expresses opinions about events or ideas in stories, poems and non-fiction; uses more than one strategy in reading unfamiliar words and establishing meaning – e.g. phonic, graphic, syntactic, contextual.

But . . .

What is a 'simple text'? There are complex narrative secrets which have to be unlocked if many minimal texts – especially in picture books – are to be read with understanding (e.g. *Rosie's Walk* (Hutchins 1968); *The Baby Who Wouldn't Go To Bed* (Cooper 1996)). The reading of pictures is a sophisticated achievement. And what does 'generally accurate' mean? Young children first need to establish the contexts and total meanings of texts (literary strategies) in order to use their wider experiences of human relationships, spoken languages (not just English), syntax, graphics and phonics.

Writing: communicates meaning in narrative and non-narrative forms using appropriate and interesting vocabulary and shows some awareness of the reader; ideas developed in a sequence of sentences; some use of capital letters and full stops; simple monosyllabic words usually spelt correctly with any inaccuracies being phonetically plausible; in handwriting, letters accurately formed and consistent in size.

But . . .

How do we define 'appropriate and interesting' vocabulary? The most creative and lively writing often breaks the 'appropriate' rule: 'My new little brother looks like a baby seal'; 'I've got cheesy maggots for my packed lunch'. The sequential development of ideas in writing is difficult for secondary pupils and adults (few people become professional writers) and the understanding of what sentences are is a complex linguistic issue and only develops with a great deal of writing and reading – this seems a tall order for the average 6- or 7-year-old. What kind of use of capital letters and full stops is required (young children delight in putting them everywhere when they first 'discover' them), and how can 'simple monosyllabic' words like 'are', 'you' or 'get' be easier to spell than distinctively shaped and richly meaningful words like 'dinosaur' and 'aeroplane'? Does accurately formed handwriting take account of left-handedness or writing experimentally in early childhood? Is any size of writing acceptable if it is consistent?

The inappropriateness of many of these National Curriculum expectations would seem to reflect a failure on the part of legislators and influential inspectors to observe young children and understand their language and literacy development, or an unwillingness to listen to early years experts. There is no doubt that we do need to nurture confidence and ability – in 'speaking and listening', for example – but this requires respect for all spoken languages and their speakers, no matter how young. It also requires adults who are good listeners as well as good talkers and are able to share with young children enthusiasm for the immense variety and excitement of daily life.

Similarly, with 'reading' we have to face up to its complexity and not underestimate or ignore the remarkable literacy activities that young children can do. Things such as speculating about the motives of story characters; talking about the authors and illustrators of books; reading the meanings and events in pictures; beginning to talk like books themselves ('once upon a time'; 'for she had nowhere to go'); predicting what might happen next in an oral or written story; and recognizing some significant letters and words and linking them with personal experience ('that says "D" like in Dinosaur Park').

'Writing' is a developmental process as well as a cultural convention, and this should be carefully observed by adults and evidence of children's thinking and problem-solving collected. This involves asking ourselves such questions as: what have the children, or this child, found out about letters and numerals?; do they 'scribble' or write in approximate lines?; how do they try to represent the sounds of the spoken language?; is there evidence of a written system that is not English?; are drawings part of the written message?; do they use capital letters, full stops, dashes, question marks?; how aware are they of who the writing is for?

We turn now from failures to set appropriate demands and expectations for the early years in the existing National Curriculum for English to the problems emerging from the recently introduced National Literacy Strategy.

The National Literacy Strategy

This government strategy was announced in 1997 to ensure that by the year 2002 80 per cent of all 11-year-olds would reach Level 4 in English of the Key Stage 2 National Curriculum tests. The strategy emerged from the consultations of a literacy task force which was not notable for the large number of early years experts it included, or co-opted, in the course of its deliberations. The task force's strategic plan includes several initiatives which are likely to have far-reaching effects on young children. The major impact however, will be through the 'literacy hour' and the linked retraining of primary teachers to put it into action.

The literacy hour

This is a key element in the literacy strategy and from September 1998 all primary schools in England were 'required' to set their targets for literacy (to reach the 2002 goal) and provide one hour of literacy teaching for every class every day. In strictly legal terms the hour and the strategy are not compulsory but schools do have a duty to teach literacy in a reasonable manner and there are clear signs that the schools inspection service will make it exceedingly difficult to avoid. The literacy hour document (DfEE 1998) is very specific about organization, content and teaching method.

The *organization* of the hour into four time slots of approximately 15, 15, 20 and 10 minutes and the specification of whole class work in the shorter slots and group work in the 20-minute period reflects a firm commitment to limiting individualized teaching and controlling, even in fine detail, what teachers do in the classroom.

The *content* of the literacy hour has a traditional linguistic flavour as it must contain work at the three 'levels' of word, sentence and text. Word-level work will include such things as phonics, spelling and vocabulary; sentence level is about grammatical awareness and punctuation; and text level involves comprehension in reading and understanding print and composition, or writing. Precise teaching objectives for each year of the primary curriculum are set down in the literacy framework for schools and this includes the Reception year which, as we know, contains many of the nation's 4-year-olds.

The *method* of teaching is one of direct instruction and the use of the time slots is tightly defined: in the first 15 minutes of the literacy hour the whole class will work on a shared text; in the second 15 minutes the whole class will do word-level work, often focused on recognizing monosyllabic words in isolation. The 20 minute session is for group work in which children either work with the teacher on guided reading in their group (all reading from copies of the same text), or work independently on reading, writing or words. Of course, the devil is in the detail and worrying questions arise about what a young child makes of group reading, or what meaningful independent word and sentence activities can be set for a 4-year-old or a 'just beginning to speak English' 5-year-old. The final 10 minutes are for the whole class to review and reflect on what has been covered in the lesson.

There may be some flexibility about doing all this in the early years, but only in terms of organization and timetabling. All the Reception year objectives must be taught systematically and whole class shared and group guided reading must be implemented from the start. Word-level work should start at the earliest stages but can be taught in groups to begin with, although teachers should introduce a full literacy hour as soon as possible and certainly by the beginning of the last term of the Reception year. Schools are encouraged to employ additional adults to support very young children, mixed age classes, children with special educational needs and children for whom English is an additional language (bilinguals) – but all must do the literacy hour.

Problems and challenges

'In the slammer'

The current initiatives and publicity about literacy and education are taking place in a highly charged atmosphere, created by linking literacy with political dogma and using the oversimplified language of crime and punishment when talking about complex issues. We hear of 'driving up' standards, of reading and literacy 'crusades' and 'revolutions', and the sending in of 'task forces'. Until very recently we were also subjected to the now notorious phrase 'zero tolerance' of failure. All these terms have appeared in documents and statements prepared by political parties and central government. The language of military expeditions, of the violent overthrow of a state, of compulsion and intolerance may make politicians and civil servants appear fashionably 'tough' but very young children who are just starting to read and write, or who have problems with literacy, are not criminals and do not deserve to be terrorized – nor can they be coerced into literacy. Similarly, teachers, carers and parents who have been bullied and harassed by 'literacy policing' and 'homework policing' provide poor models of the empowering nature of adult language, literacy and thinking for the children they care for and educate – and what can they demonstrate of the joy of learning? We need to object to this kind of language, with its accompanying attitudes, whenever and wherever we meet it.

From project to strategy

The National Literacy Project was set up in September 1996, and in January 1997 a number of English local education authorities began to trial it in their schools. It is, therefore, a very young project and still being changed and revised in the light of experience. Most educational research would expect to have a lengthy period of trial and be evaluated by independent experts (not just by the involved project schools, local education authorities, HMI and NFER) before being implemented in schools. Yet this unproven experiment has already been taken up by the government and turned into a national project which all primary schools in England were required to implement in September 1998. We do not have long-term research evidence about literacy progress among children who have done the literacy hour from age 5 to age 11, and even the January 1997 guinea piglets had completed only 19 months of national literacy project work when it became a national strategy for all!

This appears to have been a hasty, politically-driven decision and seems uncomfortably like curriculum innovation by whim and threat. This view is strengthened by the advice to teachers that they no longer need to decide *what* to teach and can get on with *doing it* (DfEE 1998).

An hour a day

On a recent trip to the USA I visited a beautifully restored nineteenth-century Vermont schoolhouse, now kept as a museum. All the textbooks and the State Syllabus for Infants were displayed and hanging on the door of the teacher's cupboard was a minute-by-minute guide to what the *teacher* should do and say, from the greeting and registering of the children in the morning, via mental arithmetic, class reading and geography, to the cleaning of slates and a final prayer. This, I realized, was the infamous nineteenth-century teacher-proof, or idiot teacher, primary curriculum (Holmes 1952), and my guess was confirmed by the curator who told me that the brightest young teachers in remote rural nineteenth-century Vermont escaped as soon as possible to the more liberal big cities where they could begin to think for themselves, improve their own education and teach with some respect for the young learners in their classrooms.

Teaching hours broken down into specific time-slots of input are dangerously close to becoming idiot teacher guidance and the plight of all our young children on the receiving end is worse than that of their teachers. They have no chance to escape and are expected to absorb what they are told, at the rate they are told it. The most interesting feature of the teaching of the literacy hour is the emphasis on a slick, polished performance by the teacher. Informal observations of Reception classes indicate that some children sitting at the front of the whole class group enjoy the teacher's 'performance' and manage a little interaction, but many who are further away drift off into contemplation of a spider under the window-sill or the writing on the T-shirt of the child next to them, or go in for more disruptive activities. This is not surprising because young children are rarely able to sit passively for an hour and many 4-year-olds do not yet understand that an adult addressing a whole class of children is also, at the same time, speaking to each individual. Furthermore, the adult at the front can have little idea of the children's interests and thoughts and probably misses all the literacy possibilities in an impromptu chorus of 'Incy Wincy Spider' or a discussion about the print on a T-shirt.

We also need to be a little cautious about taking up uncritically the impressive linguistic vocabulary used in the literacy strategy document (DfEE 1998). The references to 'levels' in the work on words, sentences and texts are based on the descriptions, or models, of language used by professional linguists. So far so good, but these levels are helpful inventions which enable linguists to describe and analyse the extremely complicated nature of spoken and written language. The levels are not really intended to be taught as true facts about language that can be discovered and then used, if we work hard enough. There is no convincing evidence that instruction in word, sentence and text levels helps young children to talk, listen, read and write with greater understanding.

Most of the work to be done in the literacy hour has already been set down in detail by *The National Literacy Strategy: Framework for Teaching* (DfEE 1998), and this means that the language the children encounter does not belong to them, or reflect their interests and experiences in any serious way. Yet most teachers of early literacy and most parents who notice their children's early language and literacy achievements are aware of how important it is that children feel some ownership and involvement in what they talk about, draw and write about, and begin to read. It is no coincidence that children start to recognize and write their own names at an early stage of emerging literacy and are pretty quick to spot the brand names of favourite foods, or are able to write their dog's name on the paved area of the nursery garden. But who owns or loves 'went', 'at' or 'is'?

It is very difficult to find worthwhile literacy activities for a class of young children to do on their own while a teacher works with a group, particularly if these activities are required to be sitting-down-paper-and-pencil activities. Many guidelines offered to teachers and many accounts by practitioners of what they are doing in the literacy hour suggest that we already have a full-blown culture of trivial pursuits in the nation's Reception and Key Stage 1 classrooms. Apparently it is now acceptable to hunt through a text for capital letters, full stops and words that have an 'h' in them – to name but a few of the exciting possibilities – and put a ring round them, or underline them! At this point it is worth going back to the previous chapter and noting the challenging real literacy which engages many nursery school and kindergarten pupils.

The requirement that the reading in the literacy hour is done in groups (guided reading), or even by the whole class with a shared text, is leading to the revival of another old-fashioned cultural experience, better known in clubs and music-halls as a community sing-song. The practice of reading round the class is being revived, with all the problems for a child of being far ahead of the rest, or well behind them, or terrified of an unknown word which is coming up, or desperately bored, confused and 'lost'. It is really saddening to try and imagine what these experiences can possibly be like for a 4-year-old who previously pored over the television listings magazines at home, read the Koran with reverence and pride, or curled up against a loving carer and shared Miffy's outings or Bernard's monster problem.

Practice divorced from principles

There is a grave danger that the rapid imposition of the literacy hour as it now stands and the insistence that teachers only have to get on and do it because the content has been decided for them, will lead to the practice of literacy teaching being completely divorced from the principles and knowledge that underpin it. The following selection of dangers should be noted by early years educators, providers, families and other carers.

The wide range of literary experiences listed by the framework, including traditional and modern stories, rhymes and poetry will be undermined if these oral and written texts are gutted for their 'sh' words, punctuation, onsets and phonemes. Quality books and poems are wasted if young readers and listeners do not learn to love them and, for example, laugh at Maisie Middleton's exploits, or sympathize with William when he tries to placate the bear under the stairs.

The research into young children's phonological awareness, or sensitivity to initial sounds (onset and alliteration) and similar end-sounds of rhyming words like 'ring', 'sing', 'king' is probably misused if we insist that young children rely on narrow phonic rules when tackling unfamiliar words. It is no use making young children learn terms like 'phoneme' and recite all 44 of them when we have not prepared them for the inconsistencies of English which has a very varied and irregular system for representing sounds in written symbols.

The well-established early years practices of shared writing and shared reading with small groups of children are not quite the same as the shared text work required in the literacy hour, although the use of large format picture and story books in the hour may appear reassuring. The focus of shared reading – as it has been practised for some years in early years settings – is on the nature of the literary experience conveyed by the text (what happens and what it means), the way in which narratives (written and pictorial) work, and how a reader behaves or sets about creating meanings from print, pictures, layout and the linking of similar personal and other literary experiences to the new text. Shared writing in good early years practice always uses the group and individual experiences of the children and turns these ideas, feelings and events into a written text. The adult writer/teacher demonstrates just what kinds of decisions a writer constantly makes and what kinds of language, print and personal knowledge can be drawn upon. The children remain in control of the message and the language, often supplying any required illustrations, while the adult scribe guides them on such matters as thinking about an audience or reader, using an appropriate form and employing spelling strategies and punctuation to good effect.

The framework for the literacy stategy also requires children to learn certain 'high frequency' words which appear in most texts and link the meanings together, but these types of words, by their very nature, only make any kind of sense in a context. The 45 words to be learnt in the Reception year (think about those 4-year-olds again) include 'we', 'and', 'am', 'it', 'the' and so forth. The only nouns in the list which could possibly be drawn, painted or modelled are 'cat', 'dog', 'dad', 'mum' and 'I', and the requirement is that these words must be known and recognized in and *out* of context. Yet it is one of the great advantages of a prolonged exposure to oral storytelling and books and print of all kinds that children learn these cohesive features of English by meeting them in meaningful contexts. One of the worst aspects of learning to read in many schools in Britain, Australia and the USA in the twentieth century has been the stumbling block of having to know the lists of isolated words at the back of reading scheme books before being allowed to get on with reading another book.

The kind of early years practice – devoid of understanding of the underlying principles of early years care and education – which we are being hurried into by recent legislation and 'persuasion' is most clearly seen in the following misunderstandings:

- young children learn by sitting for hours at a time and listening to instructions;
- the labelling of written language forms and features enables children to write and read effectively;
- doing more of the same at home every night will ensure children's educational progress;
- children's feelings, social experiences, self-esteem and some control over how and when they learn have no place in education;
- teaching is merely a matter of telling;
- once targets have been identified, learning takes place in simple, incremental stages.

A researcher has recently identified similar early years fallacies (Nutbrown 1998a), and there are encouraging signs that a growing concern about the long-term effects on young children of an early start to formal schooling will force a national review.

Early bloomers and late frosts

There is a long tradition of gardening metaphors in early years education in Europe: the kindergarten is a garden of children and the healthy mind and body were thought to be essential to learning, so the early pioneers created open-air classrooms in gardens and on verandahs. Many of these early nursery educators rescued the children they taught from poverty, semi-starvation, criminal neglect and exploitation in the slums of the cities and it is helpful to remember that 'a nursery' is also a place where young plants are nurtured! So, as we still talk of nurturing children and watching them blossom into confident young people it is not unreasonable to remind ourselves that young blooms which are forced-on too soon are often weak and likely to be struck down by a late frost.

These issues of 'too much too soon', or 'better late than early' were referred to at the end of the previous chapter and are at the heart of the Steiner Waldorf UK kindergartens' principled refusal to conform to some of the recent curriculum legislation. There is research evidence that, in the long term, a very formal start to early education damages children's social and intellectual development (Nabuco and Sylva 1996). Add to this our growing awareness that most European countries start formal schooling much later than the UK but have a comprehensive system of preschool care and education and excellent rates of adult literacy and numeracy, as well as enviable skills as speakers of two or more languages. The curriculum in the

European kindergartens avoids the early written recording of mathematics, the introduction of reading scheme books and the copying of letters and sentences because of evidence that early recording of this kind actually gets in the way of young children's understanding and thinking. The emphasis is on play and an oral curriculum which emphasizes talking, listening, discussions, storytelling, rhyme and poetry, play with the sounds of language (alliteration and rhyme again), drama, music, painting and drawing, modelling and gardening, group activities and the careful development of children's self-esteem and creativity.

Many British people had the opportunity to see this early years approach in action in a television documentary which offered some very strong criticisms of the road we appear to be going down in the UK (Channel 4 1998). Viewers had the interesting experience of seeing the utter pain and bewilderment of a Hungarian professor of child development who was struggling with the alien nature of the new British early years scene, as well as hearing the more robust comment of a Belgian kindergarten teacher that it was 'mad'! It was clear that the researchers and producers of the programme also thought that there would be 'tears before bedtime'!

These kinds of findings only make 'news' when a television programme gives them a prime-time viewing slot, but rigorous long-term research in the USA and the UK has shown quite convincingly that the advantages of a high quality informal nursery education persist into adulthood and save a society both the expense and the human waste and misery of much youth crime, truancy, drug addiction and teenage pregnancies (Ball 1994; Schweinhart and Weikart 1997). A further strengthening of this evidence is now provided by an American study on the long-term advantages of an early years and primary curriculum which emphasizes literature and the arts (Heath 1997). Children at the start of this study (30 years ago) were more likely to have had a primary education which emphasized the arts, yet these children who read more literature and did more drawing also did more writing. They did more writing in fact than their own children who have been drawn into narrower and more basic 'Three Rs' approaches in recent years. The original children from the early period of the study also proved to be more creative and flexible and happier with mathematics, science and complex ideas. The study is now looking at adolescents from low-income, multicultural, multilingual, urban backgrounds who voluntarily involve themselves in independent theatre and dance groups, and the findings are very clear. These young people stay on longer in education, have strong self-esteem and independence, win awards for achievement and good attendance at secondary school, involve themselves in community service and enjoy maths and science. Research results of this kind seem to confirm that there is an individual bonus of self-esteem associated with an early arts and humanities start to life and schooling, and that prolonged exposure to stories and literature helps children to think in a hypothetical or 'what if . . .' mode, and not be afraid of being tentative or not knowing something.

If quality early years nursery education protects young children from the late frosts of a disturbed or criminal adolescence and gives them a sense of self-worth and the ability to think independently we should want it for all children. But there is also the late frost of alienation from schooling and all things educational which blights much of our secondary school system as well as the lives of many young adults. Evidence that this begins in the very first days and weeks of infant school has been around for a long time (Barrett 1986; Bennett and Kell 1989; Sherman 1996) and it highlights the dangers of lack of individual attention, the failure of teachers to tune-in to the abilities and concerns of very young children in the first few weeks of school, and a curriculum which does not allow children to be active, involved, talkative and playful. All these negatives are currently being reinforced in the early years curriculum despite the fact that recent research into learning to read stresses the need for very careful settling-in procedures in the early days of Reception, lots of individual and small-group work with the teacher, and language and literacy experiences which are pleasurable and meaningful and respect all the literacy learning children bring to school from home (Riley 1996; Weinberger 1996).

Asking the practitioners

The curriculum requirements and frameworks outlined in this chapter have been imposed on early years settings and schools, and on the practitioners who work with the children in them, with little or no serious consultation. By serious consultation I mean a genuine invitation to debate complex issues, a willingness to listen to alternative views and an openness to change when persuaded by the experience and expertise of others. This is the democratic perspective which permeates education of good quality and unites all the books and authors in this series. So, in the best tradition of practising what one preaches I took the title of this book and turned it into a question which I sent to a number of practitioners in a variety of early years settings.

The question and the settings

This exercise was rather like a straw poll which gave me some sense of what a few practitioners who work closely with young children consider to be their top priorities in language and literacy. It is not proper research but it is a proper question to ask of any early years provider, leader, educator, nursery nurse, assistant or carer. In fact I hope that the readers of this book, whatever the nature of their responsibilities for young children, will ask it in their own local settings and schools.

It was necessary to send out two letters (see Appendix IV), one asking for permission and cooperation from the headteacher or principal of the setting and one for the practitioners in the setting which explained about the book and asked the crucial question. There had to be an additional factual question in the letter to the practitioners in order to find out the ages of the children they worked with, but the main question was: What do *you* consider to be the most important way (or ways) in which you support young children's language and literacy development?

The question was sent to three maintained nursery schools with 3- and 4-year-olds, one in rural Norfolk, one in Norwich and one in London (the school in the case study in Chapter 5), and to three First schools (covering the age range 3 to 8) in Norwich. It was also sent to a private sector Rudolf Steiner School (with a kindergarten) in Hertfordshire and staff who taught the 3- to 8-year-olds responded.

The answers

All of the settings returned some responses and a few were joint efforts by a group of teachers, classroom assistants or nursery nurses. A couple of headteachers also sent notes on their priorities for the language curriculum. Many practitioners find it threatening or just too time-consuming to write down an account of their practice and a more detailed and reliable research approach would need to offer other ways of collecting the information – using tape recorders and video cameras, or taking notes during an interview, for example.

General agreements

There was general agreement about certain aspects of the language curriculum from all the practitioners.

- Talk with other children and especially with caring and interested adults in the setting is central to children's language and literacy development.
- Just as important is the creation of a setting which is welcoming and safe and builds children's confidence and respects them and their first attempts at communicating, writing and reading.

- Pleasure (love of language is often mentioned) enjoyment and fun are important, particularly in children's early experiences of stories, poetry, rhyme and books. Some sample comments were: *'Be excited about it yourself'*; *'Encourage children to think of language as exciting'*; and *'I always think that learning should be* fun *if at all possible'*.

An early years tradition

A distinctive approach emerges from the responses of the early years practitioners in maintained nursery schools and the nursery classes and Reception years of First schools. I have called this an early years tradition as it appears to go much deeper in its principles and understandings than straightforward responses to the legislation described in the first part of this chapter. The responses emphasized:

- The creation of a literate environment in classrooms, halls and corridors, and also in the outside play space, and the provision of drawing materials, writing areas, book corners and collections of print of all kinds.
- An emphasis on talking and listening which includes the creation of small areas where children can chat; allowing time for talk with adults in a relaxed and personal way; teaching in small groups; having whole class 'circle times' for discussions; providing for lots of role play; taking children out into the community for walks and visits; and inviting visitors to come into the setting – from newborn babies to pet dogs, firefighters and senior citizens.
- A really large and attractive collection of quality books for use in the setting and for parents to borrow and read with the children at home.
- Keeping stories at the centre of the curriculum, particularly by reading to the children from books and helping children to tackle the books themselves by making story props to support their retellings (see Chapter 4).
- Encouraging the children's emerging print awareness with collections of print and introducing a range of different kinds of writing: information books, letters, invitations, first dictionaries and encyclopedias, guide books and maps, diaries and television magazines, comics and recipes.
- Keeping a strong emphasis on the poetic and musical aspects of language, especially nonsense, rhyme and play with language. Using music, rhythm, dance and singing. Making a start on fostering alphabetic and early phonological awareness.
- Supporting early writing by encouraging mark making and drawing; providing a range of tools and technologies; making books with

children and seeing them as authors. Some sample comments were: *'Resources for a literate classroom, e.g. lots of writing and words visible and having a purpose; a wide range of big books, picture books, information books, poetry and rhyme books; a quality reading area; an excellent range of books with tapes . . .'; 'Listening and talking with children – giving them time to talk and express their ideas – "tuning in" to what they are saying and the thoughts that lie behind . . .'; 'Lots of listening cues – e.g. tidy-up music, snack-time sounds. Lots of singing, chanting, body work and dance in its loosest sense! We sing everything!'; 'To begin making them aware that authors and illustrators are people, and that we too can transfer our thoughts and ideas into print'; 'A spring walk develops children's knowledge both intellectually and emotionally. It stimulates the senses and results in a fuller understanding . . . creative and written work will always be of a higher quality when children have experienced the real thing'.*

Some differences

Only one city school was constantly aware in its written responses of the children's other languages – spoken and written – and used a range of dual language texts (books with the text in another language and in English). One nursery school described a policy for inviting parents to borrow children's books for use at home, and also shared with parents information about the importance of playing about with language (nonsense, jokes and rhymes). Two nursery schools referred to helping children with special educational needs and monitoring children's individual needs carefully.

The school in the private sector had a special focus on children's emotional development and the sensory aspects of quality education. This school was the only one which had a strong focus on the importance of *telling* stories to children and although some replies did mention 'listening to stories' as important it was difficult to detect any very clear commitments and policies from other schools about adults telling stories. However, one respondent did describe the practice of oral retellings by the children of stories read to them and several had built up collections of audio story tapes.

The returns from teachers with Year 3 classes in First schools (children aged 7 and 8) were noticably narrower in their focus on literacy and listed traditional categories: *reading, phonics, comprehension, spelling, handwriting, grammar, free writing.*

It is important to treat these so-called 'differences' with great caution. These are written returns sent to me at a time of considerable overload on teachers and other practitioners and it is always easy to take the daily things we do so much for granted that we hardly think to mention them. The fact that a practice is not mentioned does not mean that it is not happening.

Supporting 24-hour literacy: a humane strategy

The case studies in Chapter 5 and the straw poll described above provide some fairly convincing evidence that early years educators are motivated by a deep concern for children and, in most cases, considerable knowledge about their development and an eagerness to learn more. Many have a deep love of language and literature which they are attempting to share with the children they work with and their families. Yet recent legislation and 'advice' appear to undermine this motivation, knowlege and professional concern, leaving practitioners feeling uncertain about their practice and increasingly obliged to do things they see as 'wrong' or 'misguided'. If we do not attempt to claim back our professionalism and responsibility for what happens in the settings we work in – and send our children to – we may damage the educational opportunities and life chances of these children.

The summary which follows is a humane strategy because it puts *people* of any age first. It also challenges the strange notion that literacy can be effectively learnt and taught in daily one-hour sessions. It is a programme for 24-hour lifelong literacy because language and its written forms pervade all our lives and all our waking hours, not to mention the impact on our dreams of what we say, hear, read and write! In the case of very young children the all-pervasiveness of language and literacy is particularly apparent because they move between homes and various care and education settings without making distinctions about 'this is learning to talk', 'this is play with words', 'this is real reading', 'this is writing', 'this is phonics' and so forth (see Figure 6.1). The distinctions they do make are likely to be of a different kind, such as 'nobody likes me', 'I don't understand', 'I'm tired', 'when do we go home?', or 'how do you draw a "H"?'.

The question of what to put in a 24-hour literacy strategy should certainly be debated by professionals and parents. One temptingly easy answer is 'everything' but a strategy, rather like a curriculum, is a selection of just some of the most highly valued practices and I have had to make my decisions about good language and literacy practices throughout this book. It is the professional duty of all carers and educators to make such choices and to learn from each other, and in that spirit I offer a reminder of four essential strategies for literacy.

Figure 6.1   The all-pervasiveness of language and literacy is apparent.

Four essential strategies

Talk, play and representation

The earlier chapters of this book have given high priority to these aspects of early development and learning: spoken language remains central to the curriculum because it shapes all our thinking, enabling us not simply to communicate with others but understand their thinking too. It is the means by which young children make sense of experiences, information and new knowledge, and talk is still one important method for teaching skills and sharing knowledge. Talk, play and representation are symbolic systems and central to the kinds of thinking which distinguish human behaviour and culture. They are all ways of letting words, pictures, gestures, clothes, rituals and many other activities – from gardening to carving totems – stand for, or represent, complex attitudes, beliefs and feelings.

Literacy depends on these basics: talk, play and representation.

Rhyme, rhythm and language patterns

Previous chapters on play with language and early literacy have empha-sized the patterns of sounds, rhythm and repetition which are usually associated with poetry. These musical qualities of any language are a major help to the young speaker who is making the move from talking to understanding print and its relationships with spoken language. For one thing, these striking and enjoyable aspects of language have the effect of making it very obvious to the child that sounds are repeated again and again, or are similar but not quite the same, or produce a musical rhythm or beat which can be tapped, clapped, stamped, danced to or sung. This makes language very obvious and an object of interest to investigate rather than a purely practical and unremarkable method of communication. Just as fine poetry can stop us in our tracks so rhymes, alliteration, rhythmic patterns of language, songs, nonsense verse and unusual words grab our attention and can make language study possible for young children.

Literacy depends on these basics: rhyme, rhythm and language patterns.

Stories and narrative

Chapter 3 set out the significance of stories and narrative in human thinking and sense-making and their role in helping children to understand particular ways of thinking and using language which are now most commonly found in books. Many encounters with told stories, picture books and story books enable children to get a hold on literary language, book language and the nature and conventions of pictures and print – including the ways in which we make meanings out of pictures and written narratives. These are important early lessons about how to be a reader.

Literacy depends on these basics: stories and narrative.

Environmental print and messages

Early lessons about what writing is for, what writers do and how print works have been described in Chapter 4. The best way to get children started on understanding that print carries messages and is available for all of us to use for our own purposes is to draw children's attention to print in their environment at every opportunity, make collections of it and spend time reading it with them. We can encourage them to play with the print, taking it apart and reassembling it, or making copies of it for their play areas, classrooms and homes. We should make a constant practice of writing and drawing messages for our children, as well as helping them to make their own meaningful marks and messages to send to a widening range of audiences.

Literacy depends on these basics: environmental print and messages.

Further reading

Edgington, M. (1998) *The Nursery Teacher in Action: Teaching 3, 4 and 5-year-olds*, 2nd edn. London: Paul Chapman.

Nutbrown, C. (1997) *Recognising Early Literacy Development: Assessing Children's Achievements*. London: Paul Chapman.

Talking together

'And how many hours a day did you do lessons?' said Alice, in a
hurry to change the subject.
'Ten hours the first day,' said the Mock Turtle: 'nine the next, and so on.'
'What a curious plan!' exclaimed Alice.
'That's the reason they're called lessons,' the Gryphon remarked:
'because they lessen from day to day.'

(Carroll [1865] 1998: 85)

It is only to be expected that a book about language development will end
where it began – by returning to the importance for all of us of communicating and talking, especially when, like Alice, we are faced with educational terminology which has not got easier to explain in the years since
1865. So the final sections of this book will focus briefly on children talking, on parents, professional carers and educators talking, and on the
crucial need for all of us to find a voice and make a difference to care and
education in the early years. (Further examples of Mock Turtles and
Gryphons talking together were difficult to find!)

Children talking

There is no intention here to repeat all the material in the first chapter of
this book, but we must never forget that babies and young children start

off as 'great communicators'. Their enormous potential for thinking and communicating is fostered and developed into the ability to speak and understand one or more languages by the simple fact that carers take them seriously, talk to them constantly as they go about the business of daily living and involve them in more and more of their activities and interests. Very young children's potential for talk is nurtured and developed by their adult carers who delight in the children's sociability, curiosity and capacity for fun. These adult carers are themselves continually rewarded and motivated by the responses of the children they live with or work with in some professional capacity. It is important to reassert these positive and optimistic claims about children's huge potential for talking and thinking and the crucial nurturing roles of the adults who first care for them. The current preoccupation with testing and ranking children, institutions and professionals is creating a tendency to think of children as potential failures and problems who might give us trouble and lower our ratings in the scramble for funds, staff or adequate 'numbers'. This is a book which, like the series of books it is part of, celebrates children and their carers and educators and seeks to share the excitement of language development – and all other aspects of child development.

Opportunities to be with other children and play with them, or alongside them, also extend the social and linguistic skills of young children and start them off on the long process of adjusting to the existence and the demands of their peers and of replacing many impulsive physical reactions with words and reasons. This is the business of thinking and mediating, rather than lashing out in blind rage, and it takes us all a long time to get it right – if we ever do! Social play with other children has other very positive linguistic and social advantages – namely, helping children to extend their own experiences, knowledge and language by allowing them to take over, imaginatively, what others know and say and add it to their own resources. This is of course the reason why lots of verbal and social interactions with adults are so stimulating and educational for young children.

The kinds of interactions that are going to be valuable and educative for children occur in genuine partnerships where each individual's contribution is welcomed and respected. When I claim that communication and talk are the foundations of all later learning and academic achievements I do have this kind of genuine talk partnership in mind. It is no easy option and demands the time and the wholehearted involvement of parents, other carers and educators. It cannot be substituted for long periods of time by formal 'lessons' in talking and listening, by 'off the shelf' courses of the 'teach your baby to talk/read/write' kind, or by sitting children in front of the 'telly'. The latter strategy is not a terrible crime and can be useful on occasions – television introduces children to some stunning visual aspects of the world and of human knowledge. However, television is not interactive in the ordinary human communicative way and babies and toddlers will not develop full language ability by watching it. The rich potential of the electronic babysitter in the corner of the room can only be brought out by adults who share viewing with children, talk to them about it, think of things to do to follow up programmes and help their children to link television experiences to their own daily lives and activities.

Parents, professional carers and educators

The welcome notice in several home languages (shown in Figure 7.1) is in the entrance of the nursery school discussed in Chapter 5 and was created by parents, nursery nurses and teachers working together and sharing their languages. It is a reminder of the fact that parents and professionals

Figure 7.1 A welcome notice, to which parents contributed.

must work together in partnerships of the genuine kind mentioned above if their children are to thrive and be successful learners in early years settings. Both case study settings in Chapter 5 had a sharp focus on partnerships between parents, educators and other carers and had policies which were constantly evolving and being adapted by all the partners involved. This dynamic partnership approach created the need to communicate well and keep on talking. Because of the complexities of adults' lives and the very demanding nature of working with young children in group settings the talk was often set down as writing to be shared between all the partners. But what a wonderful example of meaningful literacy this was for the children! The written material could be anything – personal notes and letters, regular newsletters, information about the local community, invitations to social gatherings, offers of help, resources and gifts or requests for help and advice.

The London nursery school in Chapter 5 uses its hall space as an information centre for sharing and exploring the curriculum with the children's families. This is mainly done by means of displays which use photographs, children's work and a written account to clarify 'the why' and 'the how' of what goes on in the school.

The displays are part of a shared partnership approach, not just a semi-official information service, because parents have many opportunities to talk to all the staff about this material and suggest better ways of sharing, adapting and extending it to home life and activities with their children in their particular cultural and ethnic contexts. The sharing of information about the curriculum in this school is also done through parents' albums which are loose-leaf folders in which a particular aspect of the curriculum is explained in an accessible way. Each album is lavishly illustrated with photographs of the children involved in the activity, and features examples of their work. These albums are always available to parents during the school day (see Appendix II).

The traditional parents' evenings have also changed at the nursery shool and are no longer about simply giving out information. They have become interactive workshops in which parents, carers and educators together play with the materials and resources the children use every day, listen to each other, challenge each other and explain their aspirations for the children.

Links between educators and families are very close in the Steiner Waldorf kindergartens and are often led and developed by parents who help in the schools, organize many outings and other activities, raise funds and actually make equipment for the children. In Chapter 5 mention was made of the organic vegetable garden which was being developed by parents in the Cambridge kindergarten and this activity led to simple sociable lunches together after a hard morning's digging and educating. These same parents also organized expert speakers to come and visit the school and talk about gardens of many kinds.

In the Cambridge kindergarten all parents of new children are linked up with a parent who has been involved with the kindergarten for some time and are thus drawn into their partnership relationship with the school. Staff at the school also go out into the community and share their expertise in child development, play and puppet making with local playgroup leaders, and families and children using a community centre in an adjacent deprived area.

Teachers in this kindergarten regularly share with the parents their approaches to aspects of the curriculum which may not be familiar. For example, after celebrating the Hindu festival of Diwali with the children the teachers decided to send an open letter to the parents explaining why they decided to do it and how they set about making it comprehensible to the children. The letter included the Diwali story one teacher had written for the kindergarten's celebrations and details of how they involved the children at every stage, the help provided by particular parents who celebrated the festival themselves, and an account of the events of the great day.

Finally, in this school as in the London nursery, parents' evenings are 'hands-on' events in which parents are expected to do what their children do – although with far less success! Yet these playing and learning sessions for parents and early years professionals build trust and confidence and allow the talk to flow around the important topics of learning, play, literacy, mathematical thinking, the social and emotional aspects of learning in communities, and much more.

These brief examples from the case study schools are an indication that partnerships between parents, professional carers and educators are not just about sharing information on the curriculum – they are also about social and cultural life in communities and the hopes and aspirations we all have for the young children we are involved with. This takes on huge significance if we bear in mind all the evidence which shows, again and again, that the key factor in the development of early literacy is not what schools do alone but what goes on at home, especially in the years before statutory schooling (pre-5 in the UK). The importance of home experiences to literacy and numeracy should keep us all talking together in early years settings for the sake of the children.

Finding our voices

We are in a period of massive changes and rapid upheavals in all aspects of early years care and education and it is important that parents and professionals try to look further than just the needs and concerns of their own children and settings. We have to be open and flexible and ready to learn about alternative ways of approaching the early education of our youngest citizens, particularly at this time when increasingly narrow and centralized strategies are being imposed at all levels of education. The case studies in Chapter 5 are a small contribution to the processes of valuing and learning from diversity and there are recent research and development projects which are also tackling the complex issues of working together in the early years (ECEF 1998; Hurst and Joseph 1998). The need for more flexible approaches, despite all the governmental legislation and guidance outlined in Chapter 6, is urgent because we are all parenting, caring for and educating the citizens of a twenty-first century world whose changes and complexities we can hardly predict. We can, however, be sure of one thing: the narrow certainties, superficial assessments and restricted literacies of the late nineteenth century, which have been resurrected in many features of the National Curriculum, just will not do.

Parents and professionals have to find their voices and exercise their democratic rights and responsibilities, in order to have a say in what happens to their own young children in early years settings, in order to campaign on issues which affect all families with young children, and most importantly, in order to gain access to information about alternative views and approaches to early years care and education. One example of a different approach which made national headlines and was discussed briefly in Chapter 6 is the continental European kindergarten curriculum (Channel 4, 1998). But there is also a well-established and widely researched early years curriculum promoted by educators and other professionals in the USA and the UK which is known as the Developmentally Appropriate Curriculum (DAC) (Bredekamp 1987; Blenkin and Kelly 1996) and has the central conviction that: *'education should be shaped in accord with the learners' stage of development, and the knowledge and interests which have emanated from their experiences within the home and community'* (Hurst and Joseph 1998: 39).

This developmental curriculum does not deny the value of subjects and the many branches of human knowledge, but respects learners and the ways in which they come to understand new knowledge and information by relating them to what they know and understand already. The skills of teaching, by parents and professionals, are bound up with helping young learners make these links between new and old knowledge, observing learners closely and knowing when and how to challenge them, and supporting their self-esteem and confidence so that they are never humiliated and develop the courage to 'have a go' and even 'get it wrong'.

The approach to learning language and literacy in this book has been of this developmentally appropriate kind. For example, the emphasis on communicating and talking to babies and sharing books with them, although they may not seem to be talkers and readers, and the treating of young children's marks and scribbles as written communications, are ways of affirming that the infant is already a member of the human language and literacy club and on the way to getting better at the club's activities – with a little help and encouragement from the senior members.

If we campaign in the months and years ahead for a more developmentally appropriate curriculum for the early years there are several difficult issues which must be tackled in our shared conversations and in our contributions to national debates. To start with, what should we do about the literacy strategy discussed critically in Chapter 6 and soon to be joined by a numeracy strategy? Do we really want our youngest children's delight in rhymes, stories and books distorted and channelled into silly exercises with punctuation, 'sentences' and 'phonemes' (these last two features are still debated by professional linguists and puzzle linguistics undergraduates)? Do we really feel happy about 4-year-olds regularly being taught literacy as part of a large class group, regardless of their knowledge of English or their special educational, emotional and physical needs?

Then there is the issue of partnership in education and care. Do we really believe that we can continue to build genuine partnerships between parents, educators, other professionals and local communities if parents of children as young as 4 are ordered to do 'homework' with them and given 'guidance' as to the duration of this in terms of minutes? What will happen to the respect and pride we should all take in those wonderful family reading lessons which happen anywhere and any time, as the following incident illustrates?

We are waiting for a table in a 'fast food' restaurant which uses the American system of asking customers to wait to be seated, and we are standing by the large wooden notice-board which says just that. A girl of about 5 years joins us by the notice-board and examines it intently while her mother pays at the desk for the meal they have just eaten. When her mother is ready to leave, the child pulls her towards the board and says 'Listen, mum, listen, "Please wait to be served"', pointing to the words on the notice as she reads the phrase. Mother, child and the rest of us in the queue are delighted by this demonstration, even when mum gently points out that the notice actually says, 'Please wait to be seated'. They walk off, mum saying how clever it was to get the beginning and the end of the last word right and starting to explain why the notice is about being seated rather than being served.

Another innovation likely to undermine a developmental curriculum which respects and nurtures individual learners is baseline assessment or testing. Many families, carers and early years educators are already worried about the formal requirement for baseline assessment of all children within seven weeks of arrival in a Reception class (QCA 1998). These tests to find out what children know about such things as letters, reading, phonological awareness, writing, numbers, mathematical language and personal and social development – in other words, most of the 'desirable outcomes' – will be marked and scores given for each child so that a 'baseline' is created. This baseline will eventually be used to show what learning the child achieves over the next two school years before Key Stage 1 tests at age 7. However, it is becoming clear that the individual child is not really at the centre of this particular exercise because it is mainly about what 'value' the schools themselves can claim to have 'added'. It is first and foremost a way of evaluating schools in order to rank them in league tables of school performance. The tests being used are not an adequate substitute for long-term close observations of individual children linked to carefully planned teaching strategies. Uncomfortable questions arise about the possibilities of teachers giving children only modest baseline results so that schools will appear to have added a great deal by the time the 7-year-old tests come round. Very logical questions arise about the usefulness of a national system which has already approved of more than 90 different local schemes or types of baseline tests for use in schools (QCA 1998). Surely we should expect only *one* basic baseline in a national scheme! But the most serious educational questions cluster around the moral acceptability of labelling as 'failures' or 'high achievers', or anything else, children who have not even had a chance to get started on their formal schooling. Other serious concerns centre on the untried and unproven usefulness of the tests: doubts about their suitability for such young children (most of whom will not be 5, but 4 years), and worries about schools ignoring all the valuable early learning which the assessments do not and cannot test. This includes such valuable learning and attitudes as persistence, humour, playfulness, generosity and kindness, as well as creative and unconventional thinking and problem solving, or using different cultural experiences and assumptions. These are powerful and enriching learning dispositions or attitudes and we have to ask whether the need for educators to develop flexible and detailed ways of observing and assessing young children comes a very poor second – if that – in these approaches to drawing a baseline (Nutbrown 1998b).

Looking at early years settings

Looking at early years settings – those we send our own children to, or plan to send them to, and those we work in, supervise or set up – is also part of finding our voices. Critical evaluations of our early years settings includes finding the words to describe their shortcomings and propose changes for the better. Many early years practitioners have begun to look at their own practices and set out on a process known as action research in which they implement small changes, evaluate these carefully and move on to further improvements (Blenkin and Kelly 1997). This spiral of self-improvement works best when the children's families and local community are drawn in and become part of the process too. The particular relevance of this approach for supporting language development lies in the fact – so obvious that it is frequently overlooked – that children bring the languages, stories and communicative conventions of their homes and cultures into the settings with them. This language from home is the starting point for their future academic development, their literacy and their thinking and there can be no other starting point. It is also the bedrock of their self-esteem, cultural identity and emotional stability, so any rejection or lack of respect for it will be disastrous for the children.

A visit to a setting, or any critical evaluation of one, could well start with a look at staff attitudes to the children's home language or languages, the language policy agreed on by all the practitioners in the setting and the range and variety of language, literature and literacy experiences available to the children on a daily basis – including the littlest ones in the baby room! Guidelines for doing this can be put together from the suggestions at the end of the chapters in this book and the examples of work in the case study settings in Chapter 5.

Of course we must also look at equipment and space (indoors and outside); at standards of cleanliness, safety and security; at the range of experiences and curriculum available; and at staff-children ratios and staff qualifications. But there is also the matter of 'having a vision' and this series of books is committed to a vision of early childhood learning which goes deeper than buildings, regulations and staffing. Supporting early learning emphasizes and requires respect for children as individuals; attention to equal opportunities for them to progress and develop, including equal access to good-quality early years provision; and a democratic perspective in all care and education, no matter how young and inexperienced the children in the settings (Hurst and Joseph 1998). A useful rule of thumb for assessing such important and complex features of a setting might be 'Do I feel cherished and valued here and will my child flourish here?'

Last words

This final chapter may have ranged even more widely and generally than is usual in a 'language book' but it is the privilege and the curse of language study to cross all boundaries and include just about everything. Just as we cannot separate the various aspects of language development and functions – communicating, talking, listening, reading and writing – if we are to support and nurture them effectively, so we cannot separate language from the social settings and cultures in which it is learned and shared. Similarly, we cannot separate learning to read from love of stories and books and a deepening understanding of human behaviour, history and knowledge. Most significantly for the early years, we cannot separate learning about language and literacy from how children and families feel about their languages and themselves, or how they feel about taking on new forms and functions of language, or even a new language.

Young children have so much to learn and so much to bring to the processes of learning, but they transform everything they do with their freshness of vision and their readiness to be delighted, puzzled and challenged. They bring us their new-minted language and stop us in our stale old tracks with their observations on the new worlds they have found. We have a duty to keep their language and their vision fresh and a chance – if we are prepared to learn more about the language we think we know – to share in their explorations of language and literacy. This book is a small contribution to the learning we must be prepared to do if we are to support language development in all our children.

Further reading

Barrs, M. and Ellis, S. (1998) *Reading Together Parents' Handbook*. London: Walker Books.

Hurst, V. and Joseph, J. (1998) *Supporting Early Learning: The Way Forward*. Buckingham: Open University Press.

Roberts, R. (1995) *Self-Esteem and Successful Early Learning*. London: Hodder & Stoughton.

Whalley, M. (1994) *Learning To Be Strong: Setting Up a Neighbourhood Service for Under-fives and their Families*. London: Hodder & Stoughton.

Appendix I

The Bears' Treasure Island

Chapter 1

One grey Tuesday two bears (that were born in Switzerland) were walking in Norwich, they saw a castle. They used a rope to climb in it. They saw a pig. The pig said, 'My name is Babe. What's yours?' 'My name is Berny, his is Switzerland,' said one bear. They all climbed back down. But before they get to the end of the rope it snaps. Berny and Babe fall on land. Berny twists his leg. Switzerland falls on a rock. He jumps on the next rock and jumps on land. Switzerland saves them from being shot. Babe and Switzerland carry Berny home.

Chapter 2

They all made friends with Babe, and Babe meets Ted (the leader), Electro and Ivy. Ted shows Babe his bear print machine. Ivy gets his tennis set. He finds a map on his ball. He pulls the elastic band off. Ted tells Ivy to pull the lever and get Electro. Electro tells them, 'It is a treasure map.'

Chapter 3

They get on the ship and set off, they sail for three days. Suddenly they see twenty pirate ships. 'Throw two anchors!' Shouts Ivy. One anchor falls in the sea, the other sinks a pirate ship. Ivy and Berny and Switzerland and Babe board the ship. Babe snorts in the Captain's eyes. The Captain says, 'Men, get him!!' A pirate throws a sword through Babe's collar. Babe went flying. The sword sticks in a sail. The pirates throw three darts at Babe. They miss. Berny sees Babe. Berny falls in a cannon. The cannon is lit and Berny goes flying. He falls in the sea. Switzerland and Ivy jump to Babe and Berny. They save them. They jump on their ship. They tell Electro and Ted what happened.

Chapter 4

Ted looked through a telescope and saw an island that glistened in the light. Ted tells them it is Treasure Island. They saw ten pirate ships near the island. They shoot down nine ships. They get to the island. They sail straight at the ship. It cracks in half and the pirates drown.

Chapter 5

They all get off the ship. And dig where the map says. Berny and Switzerland went down into the hole. When they said that they had found the treasure, Babe held one end of the rope and gave the other end to the bears down the hole. They tied it to the treasure chest and Babe pulled them up. They find a piece of paper that says,

TO FIND THE KEY, GO TO SEA, YOU MUST SEE,
A BIG 'T', THEN YOU WILL HAVE THE KEY.

They go to the ship. Ted reads it and says, 'We will look tomorrow.' Then they all went to bed.

Chapter 6

In the middle of the night when everyone on the ship was sleeping (except Berny and Switzerland), pirates crept on the ship. They stole the treasure. Berny and Switzerland got up, Berny tried to wake up the others, Switzerland went to stop the pirates. The others woke up. The pirates ran away.

Chapter 7

In the morning Babe, Ivy, Berny and Switzerland get off the ship. Switzerland slips on the mud into the mud. He gets out, rolls on the grass and leaves. He scares the pirates into quicksands with giant pythons and scorpions around. Switzerland washes in the sea. Berny rushes in the air and grabs the treasure. 'Bye, bye suckers!' he says to the drowning pirates.

Chapter 8

They get on the ship and sail back. The next day they get to Waterfall Island. Ivy, Switzerland, Berny and Babe get on the island. (Ivy puts some string in his jumper). Berny stops, Switzerland starts slipping down a waterfall. Berny shouts, 'Waterfall, waterfall, waterfall!!' Switzerland fell down. Babe walks in front of Berny. Berny holds on to his collar and Babe goes zooming through the water. Babe trips back on to land. Berny goes flying through the chimney of his house. Ivy uses his string to save Switzerland. He lands on Ivy. Switzerland gets up and sees the key and shouts, 'We have got the KEY!' Babe looks up and sees a rock shaped like a 'T'. When they get back to the ship they tell Ted and Electro the whole story.

Chapter 9

While the others were sailing home, Berny got a party ready. He hung up balloons around Ted's bear print machine and put honey buns, honey cake, fruit and pig food on the table. When he had finished he put a note on the door. And went to get the water.

TO TED, ELECTRO, BABE AND SWITZERLAND,
COME IN THE BEAR PRINT MACHINE.

When the others came back they looked at the note and went to the machine.

Chapter 10

They got outside, Berny said, 'We can have a party for the rest of the day!' First they played 'Pin the Tail on the Teddy' and 'Musical Teddies', 'Pig Parcel', 'Piggy in the Middle', 'Find the Pig' and other games. Then they played with the balloons. Ted moved around the machine and made bear prints. After the party they wrote a book called 'The Bears of Treasure Island' and every bear had a copy of it. They all stayed together and had adventures happily ever after.

The Teddy Team

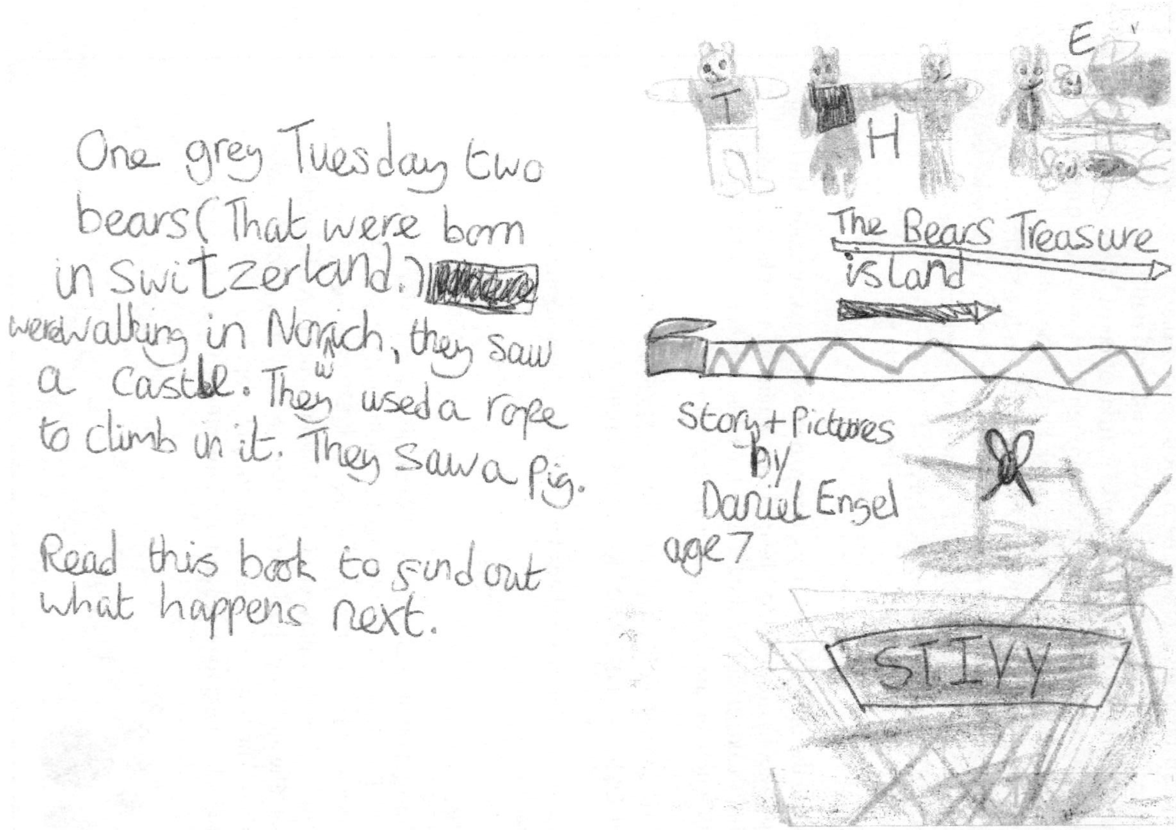

Figure AI.1 The cover of the children's book.

● ● ● Appendix II

Hampden Way Nursery School documents

Extract from a parents' album

Talking and Listening

Here at Hampden Way we have created a climate for talk which enables the children to:

discuss,
express feelings and opinions,
ask and answer questions,
give and respond to instructions,
recall experiences, real and imaginary,
describe events, processes and observations,
comment on what other people say,
argue a case,
explain ideas and respond to the ideas of others,
predict with reasons what may happen,
listen actively and recall messages,
recite a poem and sing a song,
solve problems with others,
plan actions alone or with others,
create and design new and exciting worlds,
imagine,
role-play,
communicate,

explore,
enjoy language,
investigate,
tell stories,
interview.

Planning sheet

Activity/experience	
Adult	Children
Why?	
Knowledge Attitudes Skills to be developed	
Resources required	
Language	
Evaluation	
What next?	

Child development review sheet

This is compiled throughout each child's period in the school. The areas of learning are arranged in this format so that an overall view of the child can be seen easily. The first column is a list of 'prompts' to aid comprehensive observations.

Areas of learning and experience	Significant developments	Date	Development needs and strategies
Personal and social/spiritual and moral Relationships with adults/children? Friendships? Approaches for help? Preferred activities Play (alone, parallel, collaborative) Independence, confidence Attitudes towards learning Awareness of others' needs, cultures Awe and wonder Enthusiasm, curiosity, concentration Negotiating, turn taking			
Knowledge and understanding **Science and technology** Observing, questioning, evaluating, hypothesizing, predicting Problem solving, experimenting, use of and interest in computers and machines, selection and use of materials, resources **Humanities** Interest in environment and wider community and purpose of talks about past, present and future			
Language and literacy **Speaking and listening** Initiates and listens to conversation with staff and children Use of language – descriptive, questions, follows instructions Speech vocabulary, expresses thoughts and feelings			

Areas of learning and experience	Significant developments	Date	Development needs and strategies
Reading Books – interest in, handling of: words and pictures convey meaning Recognition of letters, words, sounds Attention at story time **Writing** Mark making, pictures, symbols, interest in writing – purpose of letters			
Maths Number – counting; simple computation, songs, rhymes, games Space and shape – pattern, recognition and description Matching – 1:1 correspondence Estimating, symbols, diagrams. Comparing. Recording Mathematical language e.g. position, size Sorting and classifying. Use of maths to problem solve			
Creative and aesthetic Interest, enjoyment, appreciation, imagination Experiments, explores, feels, smells, listens, observes Appropriate use of tools Representing 2D and 3D work Storymaking. Role play Music, dance			
Physical **Gross Motor** Coordination, agility, confidence – use of static and mobile equipment Spatial awareness **Fine manipulative** Control of tools and small equipment Self care, pencil control Scissor skills Hand preference			

Appendix III

'The Five Year Old Steiner Waldorf Child' statement

The Five Year Old Steiner Waldorf Child

The curriculum which we follow provides a sound base for the development of formal skills and indeed many of our kindergarten activities are precursors to numeracy and literacy. However, our educational approach is premised on a developmental view of the child which recognises an optimum time for teaching the three Rs. This 'readiness' to learn – to be formally instructed – correlates with the process of maturation which occurs at second dentition, usually during the seventh year. Our principal approach to not forcing early literacy and numeracy means that children from Steiner Waldorf Kindergartens often enter state education without having had formal training in these areas. Naturally our kindergarten teachers and parents are concerned that bright, enthusiastic children who enter school without this training, run the risk of being labelled as 'special needs' children. The 'special gifts' or particular skills they might have acquired in a Steiner Waldorf kindergarten (or elsewhere) would simply not register on many school entry schemes. Score sheets produce overviews, unfortunately they also obscure individuality. We would ask you to bear this in mind when considering a child from one of our kindergartens.

Our own curriculum aims and objectives for the young child are as follows:-

- To recognise and support each stage of child development

- To provide opportunities for children to be active in meaningful imitation
- To provide an integrated learning experience
- To encourage learning through play
- To encourage social and moral development
- To provide a safe child-friendly environment
- To work with rhythm
- To work with parents.

A Steiner Waldorf kindergarten child will have experienced a rich variety of learning situations, all of which are related to the daily business of living. They will have had opportunities for the development of mathematics and linguistics but through integrated rather than subject-based activities. (Maths for example, might have taken place around the cooking table.) We feel that learning gains meaning and relevance by being embedded in a social context. Children will have learnt many songs, poems and stories 'by heart not head'. We place great emphasis on the oral tradition of *telling* rather than reading stories and many of our children have good aural skills, excellent memories and extended vocabularies. Our five year olds will have gained a degree of manual dexterity through activities such as sewing, drawing and painting. They will also have had plenty of opportunity for social and imaginative play which aids concentration and develops social skills. They will have learnt to care for their environment and for each other and will have experienced the importance of daily, weekly and yearly rhythms. Festivals, which deepen and enrich the experience of childhood, will have played an important part in their time at kindergarten.

(For further information see Curriculum Statement)

● ● ● Appendix IV

A *straw poll of practitioners*

January 1997

Dear Headteacher/Principal

I would be very grateful if you would distribute the enclosed research requests to all your staff (teachers, nursery nurses and classroom assistants) who work with children from 0–8 years.

The forms are self-explanatory and the returns should be anonymous, although I will be delighted to name your school or group-setting in my formal acknowledgements in the published book, if you so desire. Otherwise, the acknowledgements will only identify a city and/or region of the UK.

I can make arrangements with you to collect the completed forms after a period of about two weeks, or they can be posted to me if you prefer.

I am very aware of the burdens placed on you by National Curriculum assessments, Ofsted inspections, Nursery Vouchers, Desirable Outcomes and Baseline Assessment proposals, but I would appreciate any help you can offer.

Best wishes,
Yours sincerely

Marian Whitehead

January 1997

Dear Colleague

I am writing a book for the Open University Press on 'Supporting Language Development in the Early Years' and am keen to incorporate the views of early years professionals working with 0–8-year-olds into the text.

I am also aware that you are over-burdened and have very little time to respond to this kind of extra request, but I would greatly value your anonymous response to the two questions below. They can be returned to your Headteacher/Principal or posted direct to me, or I can arrange to collect them – after about TWO weeks.

Thank you for your time and interest.

Marian Whitehead

---

1 What is the age-range of the children you work with?

2 What do YOU consider to be the most important way (or ways) in which you support young children's language and literacy development?

(Please continue on the back of this sheet if necessary)

Bibliography

Aardema, V. and Vidal, B. (1981) *Bringing the Rain to Kapiti Plain*. London: Macmillan.

Ahlberg, J. and Ahlberg, A. (1977) *Each Peach Pear Plum*. Harmondsworth: Kestrel/Penguin Books.

Ahlberg, J. and Ahlberg, A. (1981) *Peepo*. Harmondsworth: Kestrel/Penguin Books.

Aitchison, J. (1989) *The Articulate Mammal: An Introduction to Psycholinguistics*. London: Routledge.

Aitchison, J. (1997) *The Language Web* (1996 BBC Reith Lectures). Cambridge: Cambridge University Press.

Almon, J. (1997) The importance of play as a foundation for creative thinking. Keynote address, University of Plymouth conference series 'Realizing Children's Potential: The Value of Early Learning', 6 September.

Alwyn, J. (1997) Lifting a veil on language in the kindergarten, in *Early Childhood: A Steiner Education Monograph*, pp. 16–27. Forest Row: Steiner Education UK.

Angelou, M. (1984) *I Know Why The Caged Bird Sings*. London: Virago.

Ball, C. (1994) *Start Right: The Importance of Early Learning*. London: RSA.

Barrett, G. (1986) *Starting School: An Evaluation of the Experience*. Norwich: AMMA.

Barrs, M. and Ellis, S. (1998) *Reading Together Parents' Handbook*. London: Walker Books.

Beard, R. (1995) *Rhyme, Reading and Writing*. London: Hodder & Stoughton.

Bennett, N. and Kell, J. (1989) *A Good Start? Four Year Olds in Infant Schools*. Oxford: Blackwell.

Bettelheim, B. (1976) *The Uses of Enchantment: The Meaning and Importance of Fairy Tales*. London: Thames & Hudson.

Bissex, G. L. (1980) *GNYS AT WRK: A Child Learns to Write and Read*. Cambridge, MA: Harvard University Press.

Bissex, G. L. (1984) The child as teacher, in H. Goelman, A. Oberg and F. Smith (eds) *Awakening to Literacy*. London: Heinemann.

Blenkin, G. M. and Kelly, A. V. (eds) (1996) *Early Childhood Education*, 2nd edn. London: Paul Chapman.

Blenkin, G. M. and Kelly, A. V. (eds) (1997) *Principles into Practice in Early Childhood Education*. London: Paul Chapman.

Bredekamp, S. (1987) *Developmentally Appropriate Practice in Early Childhood Programs Serving Children from Birth through Age 8*. Washington, DC: National Association for the Education of Young Children.

Bredekamp, S. and Rosegrant, T. (eds) (1992) *Reaching Potentials: Appropriate curriculum and assessment for young children*, vol. 1. Washington, DC: National Association for the Education of Young Children.

Browne, A. (1981) *Hansel and Gretel*. London: Julia Macrae.

Browne, A. (1996) *Developing Language and Literacy 3–8*. London: Paul Chapman.

Browne, E. (1994) *Handa's Surprise*. London: Walker Books.

Bruner, J. S. (1976) Nature and uses of immaturity, in J. S. Bruner, A. Jolly and K. Sylva (eds) *Play: Its Role in Development and Evolution*. Harmondsworth: Penguin.

Bruner, J. S. (1983) *Child's Talk: Learning to Use Language*. Oxford: Oxford University Press.

Bruner, J. S. (1996) A little city miracle, in Reggio Emilia *The Hundred Languages of Children*. Reggio Emilia: Reggio Children.

Bryant, P. E. and Bradley, L. (1985) *Children's Reading Problems*. Oxford: Blackwell.

Butler, D. (1979) *Cushla and Her Books*. Sevenoaks: Hodder & Stoughton.

Campbell, R. (1996) *Literacy in Nursery Education*. Stoke-on-Trent: Trentham Books.

Carle, E. (1970) *The Very Hungry Caterpillar*. London: Hamish Hamilton.

Carroll, L. ([1865]1998) *Alice's Adventures in Wonderland* and *Through the Looking-Glass*. Harmondsworth: Penguin.

Channel 4 (1998) 'Too much too soon', *Dispatches*, 29 January.

Chomsky, N. (1957) *Syntactic Structures*. The Hague: Mouton.

Chukovsky, K. (1963) *From Two To Five*. Berkeley, CA: University of California.

Claxton, G. (1997) *Hare Brain, Tortoise Mind*. London: Fourth Estate.

Cooper, H. (1993) *The Bear under the Stairs*. London: Doubleday/Picture Corgi.

Cooper, H. (1995) *Little Monster did it!* London: Doubleday/Picture Corgi.

Cooper, H. (1996) *The Baby who wouldn't go to Bed*. London: Doubleday/Picture Corgi.

Curriculum and Assessment Authority for Wales (ACAC) (1996) *Desirable Outcomes for Children's Learning Before Compulsory School Age*. Cardiff: ACAC.

DfE (Department for Education) (1995) *English in the National Curriculum*. London: HMSO.

DfEE (Department for Education and Employment) (1998) *The National Literacy Strategy: Framework for Teaching*. London: DfEE.

DfEE/QCA (Department for Education and Employment/Qualifications and Curriculum Authority) (1998) *Nursery Education: Desirable Outcomes for Children's Learning on Entering Compulsory Education*. London: DfEE/QCA.

ECEF (Early Childhood Education Forum) (1998) *Quality in Diversity in Early*

Learning: A Framework for Early Childhood Practitioners. London: National Children's Bureau.

Edgington, M. (1998) *The Nursery Teacher in Action: Teaching 3, 4 and 5-year-olds,* 2nd edn. London: Paul Chapman.

Engel, D. M. and Whitehead, M. R. (1993) More first words: A comparative study of bilingual siblings. *Early Years,* 14(1): 27–35.

Engel, S. (1995) *The Stories Children Tell: Making Sense of the Narratives of Childhood.* New York: W. H. Freeman.

EYCG (Early Years Curriculum Group) (1992) *First Things First: Educating Young Children. A Guide for Parents and Governors.* Oldham: Madeleine Lindley.

Felix, M. (1975) *The Little Mouse Trapped in a Book.* London: Methuen.

Fox, C. (1993) *At the Very Edge of the Forest: The Influence of Literature on Storytelling by Children.* London: Cassell.

Gardner, H. (1991) *The Unschooled Mind: How Children Think and How Schools Should Teach.* London: Fontana.

Goldschmied, E. and Jackson, S. (1994) *People Under Three.* London: Routledge.

Goleman, D. (1995) *Emotional Intelligence: Why it can Matter More Than IQ.* London: Bloomsbury.

Gorman, T. and Brooks, G. (1996) *Assessing Young Children's Writing: A Step by Step Guide.* London: Basic Skills Agency/NFER.

Goswami, U. and Bryant, P. E. (1990) *Phonological Skills and Learning to Read.* Hove: Lawrence Erlbaum.

Graham, A. and Gynell, D. (1984) *Arthur.* Harmondsworth: Penguin Books.

Gregory, R. L. (1977) Psychology: towards a science of fiction, in M. Meek, A. Warlow and G. Barton (eds) *The Cool Web.* London: Bodley Head.

Hall, N. (1987) *The Emergence of Literacy.* Sevenoaks: Hodder & Stoughton.

Hall, N. and Martello, J. (eds) (1996) *Listening to Children Think: Exploring Talk in the Early Years.* London: Hodder & Stoughton.

Hall, N. and Robinson, A. (1995) *Exploring Writing and Play in the Early Years.* London: David Fulton.

Halliday, M. A. K. (1975) *Learning How To Mean: Explorations in the Development of Language.* London: Arnold.

Hardy, B. (1977) Towards a poetics of fiction: an approach through narrative, in M. Meek, A. Warlow and G. Barton (eds) *The Cool Web.* London: Bodley Head.

Harris, M. (1992) *Language Experience and Early Language Development: From Input to Uptake.* Hove: Lawrence Erlbaum.

Hasan, R. (1989) The structure of text, in M. A. K. Halliday and R. Hasan (eds) *Language, Context and Text: Aspects of Language in a Social-semiotic Perspective.* Oxford: Oxford University Press.

Hayes, S. and Ormerod, J. (1988) *Eat up, Gemma.* London: Walker Books.

Heath, S. B. (1983) *Ways with Words: Language, Life and Work in Communities and Classrooms.* Cambridge: Cambridge University Press.

Heath, S. B. (1997) New directions in youth development: implications for schooling? Conference paper, Institute of Education, University of London conference series 'Literacy: From Research to Practice', 13 December.

Hill, E. (1980) *Where's Spot?* London: Heinemann.

Holmes, G. (1952) *The Idiot Teacher*. Nottingham: Spokesman.

Hoodless, P. (1996) Children talking about the past, in N. Hall and J. Martello (eds) *Listening to Children Think: Exploring Talk in the Early Years*. London: Hodder & Stoughton.

Hurst, V .and Joseph, J. (1998) *Supporting Early Learning: The Way Forward*. Buckingham: Open University Press.

Hutchins, P. (1968) *Rosie's Walk*. London: Bodley Head.

Hutchins, P. (1981) *Alfie gets in First*. London: Bodley Head.

Iannucci, A. (1998) Stir crazy, *Guardian*, 31 March.

Jeffers, S. and Chief Seattle (1991) *Brother Eagle, Sister Sky*. Harmondsworth: Penguin Books.

Jenkinson, S. (1997a) As ye sow so shall ye reap. *Steiner Waldorf Kindergarten Newsletter*, Autumn/Winter.

Jenkinson, S. (1997b) Voices on the green: the importance of play, *Early Childhood: A Steiner Education Monograph*, pp. 44–8. Forest Row: Steiner Education UK.

Jenkinson, S. (1997c) The genius of play. Conference paper, University of Plymouth conference series 'Realizing Children's Potential: The Value of Early Learning', 6 September.

Jones, R. (1996) *Emerging Patterns of Literacy: A Multidisciplinary Perspective*. London: Routledge.

Kent, G. (1997) Information technology: exploiting the learning potential with early years children. *Early Childhood Review: Papers from GAEC*, 4: 4–8.

Kress, G. (1997) *Before Writing: Rethinking the Paths to Literacy*. London: Routledge.

McArthur, T. (1995) Rhythm, rhyme and reason: the power of patterned sound, in R. Beard (ed) *Rhyme, Reading and Writing*. London: Hodder & Stoughton.

Matthews, J. (1994) *Helping Children to Draw and Paint in Early Childhood. Children and Visual Representation*. London: Hodder & Stoughton.

Medlicott, M. (1997) Storytelling: the essential art of speaking and listening. Workshop seminar, Institute of Education, University of London conference series 'Developing language in the Early Years', 23 June.

Miller, L. (1996) *Towards Reading*. Buckingham: Open University Press.

Moore, R. S. and Moore, D. N. (1975) *Better Late Than Early: A New Approach for your Child's Education*. New York: Reader's Digest Press.

Morris, D. (1991) *Babywatching*. London: Jonathan Cape.

Nabuco, E. and Sylva, K. (1996) The effects of three early childhood curricula on children's progress at primary school in Portugal. Paper presented at ISSBD Conference, Quebec, unpublished.

Nelson, K. (1989) *Narratives from the Crib*. Cambridge, MA: Harvard University Press.

Newkirk, T. (1984) Archimedes' Dream. *Language Arts,* 61(4): 341–50.

Nutbrown, C. (1997) *Recognising Early Literacy Development: Assessing Children's Achievements*. London: Paul Chapman.

Nutbrown, C. (1998a) *The Lore and Language of Early Education*, USDE Papers in Education. Sheffield: University of Sheffield.

Nutbrown, C. (1998b) Early assessment: examining the baselines. *Early Years,*19(1): 50–61.

Ofsted (Office for Standards in Education) (1997) *The Quality of Education in Nursery Voucher Settings*. London: HMSO.

Opie, I. and Opie, P. (1959) *The Lore and Language of Schoolchildren*. Oxford: Oxford University Press.

Paley, V. G. (1981) *Wally's Stories: Conversations in the Kindergarten*. Cambridge, MA: Harvard University Press.

Paley, V. G. (1986) *Mollie is Three: Growing Up in School*. Chicago: University of Chicago Press.

Payton, S. (1984) Developing awareness of print: a young child's first steps towards literacy, *Education Review Offset Publication No. 2*, Birmingham: University of Birmingham.

Pinker, S. (1994) *The Language Instinct: The New Science of Language and Mind*. Harmondsworth: Allen Lane/Penguin.

Potter, B. ([1908] 1989) The Tale of Jemima Puddle-Duck, in *The Complete Tales of Beatrix Potter*. London: F. W. Warne.

QCA (Qualifications and Curriculum Authority) (1998) *The Baseline Assessment Information Pack: Preparation for Starting Baseline Assessment*. London: QCA.

Rawson, M. (ed.) (1997) *Steiner Waldorf Education: Aims, Methods and Curriculum*. Forest Row: Steiner Education UK.

Reddy, V. (1991) Playing with others' expectations: teasing and mucking about in the first year, in A. Whiten (ed.) *Natural Theories of Mind*. Oxford: Blackwell.

Reggio Emilia (1996) *The Hundred Languages of Children: A Narrative of the Possible* (catalogue of the exhibit). Reggio Emilia: Reggio Children.

Riley, J. (1996) *The Teaching of Reading: The Development of Literacy in the Early Years of School*. London: Paul Chapman.

Roberts, R. (1995) *Self-Esteem and Successful Early Learning*. London: Hodder & Stoughton.

Rosen, B. (1991) *Shapers and Polishers: Teachers as Storytellers*. London: Mary Glasgow.

Rousseau, J. J. ([1762] 1991) *Emile*. London: Dent.

SCAA (School Curriculum and Assessment Authority) (1996) *Nursery Education: Desirable Outcomes for Children's Learning on Entering Compulsory Education*. London: DfEE.

Schaffer, H. R. (ed.) (1977) *Studies in Mother-Infant Interaction*. London: Academic Press.

Schweinhart, L. and Weikart, D. (1997) *Lasting Differences: The High/Scope Pre-school Curriculum Comparison Study Through Age 23*. Ypsilanti: High Scope Press.

Scrivens, G. (1995) 'Where's the 'K' in emergent literacy?': nursery children as readers and writers. *Early Years*, 16(1): 14–19.

Sendak, M. (1967) *Where the Wild Things Are*. London: Bodley Head.

Sherman, A. (1996) *Rules, Routines and Regimentation: Young Children Reporting on their Schooling*. Nottingham: Educational Heretics Press.

Smith, B. H. (1981) Narrative versions, narrative theories, in W. J. T. Mitchell (ed.) *On Narrative*. Chicago: University of Chicago Press.

Smith, F. (1988) *Joining the Literacy Club*. London: Heinemann.

Steptoe, J. (1987) *Mufaro's Beautiful Daughters*. London: Hamish Hamilton.

Stern, D. (1977) *The First Relationship: Infant and Mother.* London: Fontana.

Tizard, B. and Hughes, M. (1984) *Young Children Learning: Talking and Thinking at Home and at School.* London: Fontana.

Torrey, J. W. (1973) Illiteracy in the ghetto, in F. Smith (ed.) *Psycholinguistics and Reading.* New York: Holt, Rinehart and Winston.

Trevarthen, C. (1993) Playing into reality: conversations with the infant communicator. *Winnicott Studies*, 7: 67–84.

Vipont, E. and Briggs, R. (1969) *The Elephant and the Bad Baby.* London: Hamish Hamilton.

Vygotsky, L. S. (1978) *Mind in Society: The Development of Higher Psychological Processes.* Cambridge, MA: Harvard University Press.

Wade, B. and Moore, M. (1993) *Bookstart in Birmingham.* London: Book Trust.

Wade, B. and Moore, M. (1996) Children's early book behaviour. *Educational Review*, 48(3): 283–8.

Wade, B. and Moore, M. (1997) Parents and children sharing books: an observational study. *Signal*, 84: 203–14.

Wagner, J. and Brooks, R. (1977) *John Brown, Rose and the Midnight Cat.* Harmondsworth: Penguin Books.

Weddell, C. and Copeland, J. (1997) The bad news: TV your children really watch, *The Australian*, 18 September.

Weinberger, J. (1996) *Literacy Goes To School: The Parents' Role in Young Children's Literacy Learning.* London: Paul Chapman.

Weir, R. H. (1962) *Language in the Crib.* The Hague: Mouton.

Wells, G. (1987) *The Meaning Makers: Children Learning Language and Using Language to Learn.* Sevenoaks: Hodder & Stoughton.

Whalley, M. (1994) *Learning To Be Strong: Setting Up a Neighbourhood Service for Under-fives and Their Families.* London: Hodder & Stoughton.

White, D. (1954) *Books Before Five.* New Zealand: NZ Council for Educational Research.

Whitehead, M. R. (1990) First words: the language diary of a bilingual child's early speech. *Early Years*, 10(2): 53–7.

Whitehead, M. R. (1996) *The Development of Language and Literacy.* London: Hodder & Stoughton.

Whitehead, M. R. (1997) *Language and Literacy in the Early Years*, 2nd edn. London: Paul Chapman.

Winnicott, D. W. (1971) *Playing and Reality.* Harmondsworth: Penguin.

Zipes, J. (1979) *Breaking the Magic Spell: Radical Theories of Folk and Fairy Tales.* London: Heinemann.

Index

READ IT TO ME NOW! (SECOND EDITION)
LEARNING AT HOME AND AT SCHOOL

Hilary Minns

- What do young children from different cultural backgrounds learn about reading and writing before they come to school?
- How can schools work with parents to incorporate children's pre-school literacy learning into policies for the development of literacy?
- What strategies can early years' teachers use to support young children's understanding of the reading process?

Read it to me now! charts the emergent literacy learning of five 4-year-old children from different cultural backgrounds in their crucial move from home to school, and demonstrates how children's early understanding of reading and writing is learnt socially and culturally within their family and community. Drawing the children's stories together, Hilary Minns discusses the role of the school in recognizing and developing children's literacy learning, including that of emergent bilingual learners, and in developing genuine home–school links with families. This edition of *Read it to me now!* makes reference to current texts that take knowledge and ideas of children's literacy learning further, and includes discussion of the literacy require-ments of the National Curriculum.

Contents
Introduction – Part 1: Five children – Gurdeep – Gemma – Anthony – Geeta – Reid – Part 2: Further considerations – Learning to read – The role of story in young children's lives – Reading partnerships – Pathways to reading – References and further reading – Index.

176pp   0 335 19761 2 (Paperback)   0 335 19762 0 (Hardback)

TOWARDS READING
LITERACY DEVELOPMENT IN THE PRE-SCHOOL YEARS

Linda Miller

- How can teachers, nursery nurses and child-care workers ensure that pre-school children develop essential literacy skills?
- What role can parents play?
- Can children's home experiences be built upon in the classroom or nursery?

This book brings together recent research on early literacy development and presents it accessibly to answer these and other questions. All aspects of early literacy development are considered – the development of skills necessary for later success in reading and writing, including the importance of rhyme and environmental print.

A theme which runs throughout the book is that parents and professional educators need to work in partnership. Linda Miller describes a range of recent projects which have involved parents in their young children's literacy development and offers practical suggestions for implementing such projects. Strategies for observing, recording and providing for young children's literacy development in a wide range of pre-school and early years settings are also discussed.

The book will be valuable reading for anyone working with young children in pre-school and early years settings and will also be of great interest to parents.

Contents
Introduction – The emergency of literacy – Towards reading: what children come to know – Towards Writing: what children come to know – The role of parents in literacy development – Family literacy – Sharing books in the pre-school: what children learn – Parents as partners: setting up a literacy project – Observing and recording early literacy development – Provision for literacy in the pre-school – The supporting adult – Continuity between home and pre-school – References – Index.

144pp   0 335 19215 7 (Paperback)   0 335 19216 5 (Hardback)

READING IN THE EARLY YEARS HANDBOOK

Robin Campbell

Reading in the Early Years Handbook is a reference text covering all aspects of young children learning to read. It deals with a comprehensive list of topics ranging from *apprenticeship approach* to *nursery rhymes* to *whole language*. The text also deals with organizational issues such as *classroom management* and *time for literacy*. In all, some sixty topics are presented alphabetically and each of these topics is followed by suggestions for further reading. Additionally, several topics have 'In the classroom' sections where examples from the classroom are used to highlight the particular issues. The comprehensive material is presented in a handbook format to enable easy access for readers.

Contents

Introduction – Apprenticeship approach – Assessment – Audience – Big books – Breakthrough to literacy – Bullock Report – Classroom management – Classroom organization – Classroom print – Computers – Conferencing – Cue systems – Discussions – Emerging literacy – Environmental print – Formula for beginning reading – Genres – Hearing children read – Home–school links – Illustrations – Invented spelling – Knowledge about language – Language experience approach – Left-to-right directionality – Library corner – Listening area – Methods – Miscue analysis – National Curriculum – Nursery rhymes – Organic vocabulary – Paired reading – Phonemic awareness – Phonics teaching – Play activities – Punctuation – Reading drive – Reading non-fiction – Reading recovery – Reading schemes – Real books – Real books approach – Record-keeping – Responding to miscues – Running records – Scanning and skimming – School policy – Shared reading – Standard Assessment Tasks – Story grammar – Story readings – Sustained silent reading – Teacher's role – Text-to-life connections – Thematic work/topic work – Time for literacy – Whole language – Writing – Writing centre – Your classroom – References.

192pp   0 335 19309 9 (Paperback)